On the Altar of Freedom

On the

A Black Soldier's

Altar of

Civil War Letters

Freedom

from the Front

Corporal James Henry Gooding

Edited by Virginia Matzke Adams

Foreword by James M. McPherson

The University of Massachusetts Press

Amherst

This book is published with the support and cooperation of the University of Massachusetts at Boston.

Copyright © 1991 by
The University of Massachusetts Press
All rights reserved
Printed in the United States of America
LC 91–39
ISBN 0–87023–745–4
Set in Century Expanded
Printed and bound by Thomson-Shore

Frontispiece. Study for head of a black soldier by Augustus Saint-Gaudens. Courtesy, Saint-Gaudens National Historical Site and Sidney Kaplan.

Library of Congress Cataloging-in-Publication Data

Gooding, James Henry, 1837–1864.
   On the altar of freedom : a black soldier's Civil War letters from the front / James Henry Gooding; edited by Virginia Matzke Adams; foreword by James M. McPherson.
   p.   cm.
   Includes bibliographical references and index.
   ISBN 0–87023–745–4 (alk. paper)
   1. Gooding, James Henry, 1837–1864—Correspondence.   2. United States. Army. Massachusetts Infantry Regiment, 54th (1863–1865)—Biography.   3. United States—History—Civil War, 1861–1865—Participation, Afro-American.
   4. Massachusetts—History—Civil War, 1861–1865—Participation, Afro-American.
   5. Afro-Americans—Massachusetts—New Bedford—Correspondence.   6. Soldiers—Massachusetts—New Bedford—Correspondence.   7. New Bedford (Mass.)—Biography.   I. Adams, Virginia M.
   II. Title
   E513.5 54th .G66   1991
   973.7'415'092—dc20
   [B]   91–39
   [92]   CIP

British Library Cataloguing in Publication data are available.

For honor, duty, and liberty.

James Henry Gooding
April 18, 1863

Contents

Illustrations

Foreword

James M. McPherson

In 1863 the Fifty-fourth Massachusetts Volunteer Infantry became one of the Civil War's most famous regiments. On July 18 of that year, the Fifty-fourth spearheaded an assault on Fort Wagner, a Confederate earthwork protecting the entrance to Charleston Harbor. Part of an unsuccessful Union campaign to capture Charleston, this attack on Fort Wagner was repulsed. This was not unusual for frontal assaults against fortified defenses in the Civil War. Nor were the nearly 50 percent casualties suffered by the Fifty-fourth extraordinary. What *was* notable about this event was the color of the Union soldiers. The Fifty-fourth was a black regiment—one of the first such units raised in the North, and thereafter the most renowned of the 166 black regiments that by war's end had served in the Union army.

The assault on Fort Wagner was, in the romantic rhetoric of the Victorian era, "a glorious failure." This image provided the title for the powerful movie *Glory*, which dramatized the story of the Fifty-fourth and its youthful white colonel, Robert Gould Shaw, who was killed leading the charge on Fort Wagner. Shaw did not die in vain (to continue the Victorian idiom), nor did the men who fell with him. For if in a narrow sense the attack was a failure, in a more profound sense it was a success of historic proportions. The unflinching behavior of the regiment in the face of an overwhelming hail of lead and iron answered the skeptic's question, "Will the Negro fight?" It demonstrated the manhood and courage of the race to millions of white people in both North and South who had doubted whether black men would stand in combat against soldiers of the self-styled master race. It ensured the permanence of the policy of enlisting black soldiers, which until then had been regarded as a dubious experiment.

The experiment had been launched in the fall of 1862. Once the Lincoln administration committed itself to emancipation as a war policy of weakening the Confederacy by promising liberation to its enslaved labor force, the Union government took the next logical step. It decided to enlist part of that liberated labor force in the Union army. In Louisiana, Kansas, and South Carolina this effort went forward slowly amid continuing skepticism about the potential of black soldiers. In May 1863 the *New York Tribune*, the North's most powerful newspaper and a supporter of black enlistment, noted that "loyal whites have generally become willing that [blacks] should fight, but the great majority have no faith that they will do so. Many hope they will prove cowards and sneaks—others greatly fear it." Black soldiers *did* fight well on a few occasions in the first half of 1863. But white doubts persisted, and most black units were restricted to duty as labor battalions or rear-area garrison personnel.

In January 1863, Governor John Andrew of Massachusetts finally succeeded in his quest for permission to recruit the first regiment to be composed mainly of northern free blacks. This became the Fifty-fourth. A principled antislavery man himself, Andrew was determined to appoint officers "of firm antislavery principles . . . superior to a vulgar contempt for color." In Robert Gould Shaw, a twenty-six-year-old Harvard alumnus, son of prominent abolitionist parents, and a combat veteran of nearly two years in white regiments, Andrew found his colonel to shape and train the regiment.

When the Fifty-fourth arrived at the fighting front on the South Carolina coast in June 1863, Shaw's first battle was for the chance to fight—rather than unload lumber, dig trenches, and police camps. At Fort Wagner on July 18, his men got the opportunity they wanted. Their courage ended all doubts about the "experiment" of black soldiers. "Who asks now in doubt and derision, 'Will the Negro fight?'" commented one abolitionist. "The answer is spoken from the cannon's mouth . . . it comes to us from those graves beneath Fort Wagner's walls, which the American people will surely never forget." At the war's end the *New York Tribune* pronounced a true verdict: "It is not too much to say that if this Massachusetts Fifty-fourth had faltered when its trial came, two hundred thousand colored troops for which it was a pioneer would never have been put into the field. . . . It made Fort Wagner such a name to the colored race as Bunker Hill has been for ninety years to the white Yankees."

Coming at the same time as the draft riots in New York City, where white mobs inflamed by a racist Democratic press attacked blacks, Republicans, draft offices, and other symbols of Union authority, the Fifty-fourth's heroic behavior quickened a transformation in northern opinion. Many Republican spokesmen pointed out the moral: Black men who fought for the Union deserved more respect than white men who rioted against it. As usual, President Lincoln said it best. In a public letter written a month after the assault on Fort Wagner, he told opponents of emancipation that when Union victory in this war finally brought a new birth of freedom to the United States, "there will be some black men who can remember that, with silent tongue, and clenched teeth, and steady eye, and well-poised bayonet, they have helped mankind on to this great consummation; while, I fear, there will be some white ones, unable to forget that, with malignant heart, and deceitful speech, they have strove to hinder it."

The Fifty-fourth's fighting career did not end with the assault on Fort Wagner. The regiment fought on through the rest of the war in the South Carolina and Florida theaters. The remarkable record of the Fifty-fourth from training camp to the battle of Olustee (Florida) in February 1864 is chronicled by the extraordinary series of letters published in this book. Civil War bookshelves are replete with volumes of letters written by white soldiers. But published letters by black soldiers are rare; these letters printed weekly in a Massachusetts newspaper over the period of a year are unique. And they are not run-of-the-mill soldier letters. The author, a corporal in the Fifty-fourth, was observant, well informed, a fluent writer, passionately committed to the cause of Union, liberty, and black rights. He also possessed a sense of humor that makes these letters a delight as well as an education to read. James Henry Gooding fought at Fort Wagner, and he describes the terrors and heroism of that battle. He chronicles the marches, skirmishes, picket duty, and trench warfare engaged in by his regiment. He also describes camp life, exhausting duty in blistering heat and freezing cold, bad food and Thanksgiving feasts, insects, sickness, suffering, laughter, and male camaraderie that made up a soldier's life. The letters also provide a fine account of the effort to capture Charleston in 1863. Slighted in many histories of the Civil War because it accomplished no strategic success, this campaign nevertheless attracted a great deal of attention at the time and absorbed a significant portion of Union resources.

Gooding's letters protested the discrimination in pay between white

and black soldiers that prevailed until 1864 because the law that specified their pay had been enacted on the assumption that blacks would
perform labor rather than combat duty. This "is an unjust distinction to
men who have only a black skin to merit it," wrote Gooding. "To put the
matter on the ground that we are not soldiers would be simply absurd. . . . Too many of our comrades' bones lie bleaching near the walls
of Fort Wagner to subtract even one *cent* from our hard earned pay. . . .
[This] injustice . . . rob[s] a whole race of their title to manhood, and
even make[s] them feel, no matter how faithful, how brave they had
been, that their mite towards founding liberty on a firm basis was
spurned, and made mock of."

Gooding's eloquence helped persuade Congress to equalize the pay of
white and black soldiers in 1864. But this came too late to benefit him.
Wounded and captured at the battle of Olustee on February 20, 1864,
Gooding was imprisoned at Andersonville where he died in July—one
of the thirteen thousand Union prisoners of war (nearly all of them
white) who died in that most notorious of prison camps.

Virginia Adams has done a superb detective job of tracking down
information about Gooding and other persons mentioned in his letters.
Her annotations provide a major contribution to Civil War scholarship.
But the letters themselves are the most important contribution. They
open a window that lets us see the war more clearly through the eyes of
a black soldier who gave his life in the terrible but noble conflict that
freed the slaves and preserved the existence of the United States. With
the publication of these letters, our understanding of the Civil War is
immeasurably richer.

Introduction

Virginia Matzke Adams

On February 9, 1863, John A. Andrew, governor of Massachusetts, wrote to James B. Congdon of New Bedford saying that he was beginning to organize and recruit a regiment of colored men to be called the Fifty-fourth Regiment of Massachusetts Volunteers. "It is my design and hope," he continued, "to make this a *model* regiment and, as it will be the first so raised, it is my intention to make it the *best*. . . ."

After outlining plans for recruiting the officers, Governor Andrew asked Congdon to become a corresponding member of a committee to support recruitment and organization of the regiment. He added, "Your long and well-known interest in ideas which now unite patriotism and philanthropy where they belong in a common work has encouraged me to write this note."[1]

The person to whom Andrew wrote was well disposed to accept the governor's invitation. James Bunker Congdon, one of New Bedford's most prominent civic leaders, had been a founding member of the New Bedford Anti-slavery Society in 1834 and a quiet champion of black civil rights on more than one occasion. A banker, he had served the town and, after its incorporation in 1847, the city for thirty years, first as a selectman, then as president of the Common Council, and later as city treasurer. His most visible achievement, and the one in which he probably took the most satisfaction, was the establishment of the New Bedford Free Public Library; yet, according to one writer, there was no philanthropic movement in the community that did not receive his active support.[2]

1. Governor John A. Andrew, War Correspondence, Executive Letters Sent, 1861– 1865, 12: 483, at Commonwealth of Massachusetts Military Division History Research and Museum, Natick. (Hereafter referred to as Letters Sent.)

2. G. H. D. in Leonard Bolles Ellis, *The History of New Bedford and Its Vicinity* (Syracuse, N.Y., 1892), p. 85 in Appendix.

The project to recruit, train, and arm black soldiers for service against the South was one in which Governor Andrew had long been interested. And northern blacks had offered their help on several occasions. Since 1792, however, there had been a federal prohibition against enlisting blacks in state militias, and by custom blacks had never been accepted in the regular army.

At the beginning of the war there was no apparent need to enroll black troops. In the first months after the fall of Fort Sumter, it was believed that the conflict would soon be over. Volunteers were asked to enlist for just three months, and men readily signed on with a patriotic fervor that was augmented by promises of generous bounties. Later, as the war dragged on and Union losses mounted, joining up for the longer term which was then required was not such an attractive proposition, and it became necessary to find ways to increase the number of enlistments.

From the beginning, President Lincoln and most Northerners had seen the conflict as a struggle to preserve the union and not as a war to abolish slavery. The effort to keep the border states from joining the South in secession meant, so it was believed, accepting slavery in the states where it already existed. As long as this policy prevailed, arming fugitive slaves could only be seen as fomenting slave insurrection, and recruiting free blacks while others remained in bondage would be impossible.

The arming of blacks was therefore not considered an option. It was felt by many that blacks would not make good soldiers, that they lacked the courage to fight, and that white troops would refuse to serve with them. There was also fear that the reaction in the South and in the border states might prolong the war.

Nevertheless, by midsummer 1862 circumstances were forcing the issue. Union troops in the South were attracting large numbers of slaves who had fled from their owners and were seeking refuge and freedom in the Union camps. As the property of belligerents they were declared "contraband" and Congress passed an article of war forbidding their return to their former masters.[3]

3. The date was March 13, 1862 (James M. McPherson, *Battle Cry of Freedom: The Civil War Era* [New York, 1988], 497).

Since this swelling tide of refugees put an ever-greater strain on Union resources, it seemed only sensible to take advantage of the extra manpower. A regiment of free Negroes had already been formed in Louisiana, and one that included contrabands was being organized in Kansas, when Congress passed the Militia Act of July 17, 1862, authorizing enrollment of Negroes in "any military or naval service for which they may be found competent." In the fall, three more regiments were organized, two in Louisiana and one, led by Bostonian Thomas Wentworth Higginson, in South Carolina. Six months later the Emancipation Proclamation not only freed the slaves in belligerent territory as an "act of justice," but sanctioned the use of blacks in the federal armed forces as well.[4]

The war was about slavery after all, and those who had most to gain from a Union victory were going to be allowed to make their contribution toward that end. In late January 1863, the governor of Massachusetts extracted permission from Washington to raise the first regiment of free Negroes in the North.

Within the next two weeks Governor Andrew recruited his commanding officer, Robert Gould Shaw, and second-in-command, Norwood P. Hallowell, along with several of the line officers. The men had been measured against a high standard: "I am desirous to have for its officers," Andrew wrote to Shaw's father, "—particularly for its fieldofficers—young men of military experience, of firm antislavery principles, ambitious, superior to a vulgar contempt for color, and having faith in the capacity of colored men for military service. Such officers must necessarily be gentlemen of the highest tone and honor; and I shall look for them in those circles of educated antislavery society which, next to the colored race itself, have the greatest interest in this experiment." Of the twenty-nine officers selected, all but five were veterans drawn from other regiments, and six had held previous commissions. Their average age was about twenty-three.[5]

Meanwhile, Governor Andrew's committee in support of the Fifty-

4. Ibid., 563–64.
5. Luis F. Emilio, *History of the Fifty-fourth Regiment of Massachusetts Volunteer Infantry, 1863–1865* (Boston, 1894; New York, 1968), 3, 6. (Subtitle: *A Brave Black Regiment*).

fourth had begun its work. Within a short time the sum of $5,000 was raised,[6] and altogether the committee collected nearly $100,000 to meet expenses that included transportation and board for recruits. George L. Stearns was appointed agent for the committee. He soon established recruiting stations from Boston to St. Louis, for although the 1860 census had shown that there were 1,973 free colored males of military age in Massachusetts, there was agreement from the outset that recruiting efforts would have to be made in other states as well.[7]

In New Bedford, Lieutenant James W. Grace opened an office downtown on William Street on February 10.[8] The city was thought to be particularly fertile ground for any recruiting effort since there was a large community of educated and articulate African Americans living there.[9] Ten days after the fall of Fort Sumter in 1861, a group of these black citizens had met at City Hall to discuss a course of action and had adopted the following resolutions:

Whereas, In view of the probable departure from our city within a short time of a large portion of our patriotic military companies, called out for the defense of our common country, in which case the citizens of New Bedford would naturally have a feeling of insecurity for their persons and property in the excited state of the public mind incident upon the existence of actual war, therefore,

Resolved, That as true and loyal citizens (although exempt by law from military duty,) we hold ourselves in readiness to organize military companies to be officered and equipped, and to drill regularly for the protection and maintenance of peace and good order, and for the security and defence of our city and State against any and all emergencies.

6. Congdon reported to Governor Andrew on Feb. 16, 1863, that the New Bedford Citizens' Fund Committee had voted to make available $1,000. (Massachusetts Archives at Columbia Point, Executive Department Letters, 1862–1863, vol. 57a, no. 49).

7. Dudley Taylor Cornish, *The Sable Arm: Negro Troops in the Union Army, 1861–1865* (New York, 1956), 107.

8. James William Grace, a native of Maine who had been a merchant in New Bedford for twelve years, had no previous military experience.

9. According to the 1860 census in Massachusetts, New Bedford's black population of 1,518 persons was second only to Boston's, and the largest relative to the total population of the city.

Resolved, That the proceedings of this meeting be laid before the Mayor of this city and the Governor of this State, and we pledge them four hundred men that will fight for liberty, to be ready at any moment to rally to their support wherever our services may be required.[10]

Although the offer was not accepted in 1861, that patriotic sentiment would be called upon in 1863. Lieutenant Grace visited black churches in the city and explained the need. He invited persuasive speakers such as William Lloyd Garrison, Wendell Phillips, and Frederick Douglass to address meetings. They knew the city well, having spoken there often before the war.

Douglass, of course, had lived in New Bedford for three years when he first fled from the South a quarter of a century earlier. In describing that time, he spoke of his surprise at seeing how well blacks lived in New Bedford. His friend Nathan Johnson "lived in a neater house; dined at a better table; took, paid for, and read, more newspapers; better understood the moral, religious, and political character of the nation,—than nine-tenths of the slaveholders in Talbot County, Maryland."[11]

New Bedford, the whaling capital of the world, was a prosperous city in the decades before the war, wealthier than any other city of comparable size in the country. The whaling industry provided ample work on the waterfront and on whaleships and ample returns in the counting houses. The city was cosmopolitan. From its harbor, ships had sailed to most of the world's ports, and its whalemen had often been the first to visit and report on unknown and exotic places. On its streets, one could encounter representatives of many different races and cultures—Portuguese and other Europeans, Africans, Asians, Polynesians, perhaps even an Eskimo or two.

Within the black community of New Bedford there were many different strands. There were descendants of African blacks brought to New England as slaves, who later earned or were given their freedom. Some of these had married Indians from the local Wampanoag commu-

10. New Bedford *Standard*, April 24, 1861.
11. Frederick Douglass, *Narrative of the Life of Frederick Douglass, An American Slave* (New York, 1968), 116.

nities. There were Africans from the Cape Verde Islands who had joined crews of whaling vessels and later settled in New Bedford. There were West Indians who annually gathered on August 1 to commemorate the British emancipation of the islands (in 1834), with a parade, speeches, and a gala picnic.[12] And there were runaway slaves from the South who, like Frederick Douglass, had found New Bedford both a sanctuary and a springboard for a new life of freedom and economic independence.

The tone of the city was set initially by its Quaker founders at the end of the eighteenth century. Industrious, thrifty, honest, and benevolent, they were descended from pioneers of the anti-slavery movement in this country. As early as 1715, the Dartmouth Monthly Meeting had urged the Rhode Island Quarterly Meeting to decide whether Friends should own slaves or participate in the trade. Both the Dartmouth and Nantucket meetings were opposed to slaveholding, although it was not until much later that their views prevailed in Massachusetts.[13]

Frederick Douglass had been impressed with the way in which the blacks of New Bedford were willing to speak up for their rights and even to fight for them. That was a quality of spirit dating back at least to 1788, the year in which Paul Cuffe, his brother, and others went before the General Court of Massachusetts to petition for exemption from taxation on the grounds that they were poor and had few of the rights and privileges of white people. The petition failed, but Cuffe went on to become a successful shipping merchant, a Quaker philanthropist, and a black Yankee without peer, who did business and even dined with some of the leading citizens in this country and abroad.[14]

Nevertheless, as the nineteenth century advanced, New Bedford was not without prejudice and many aspects of life there were segregated. The caulkers refused to work alongside Douglass in 1838. Railroads, steamboats, and even churches had separate seating for blacks. In 1845, a black man was turned down for membership in the New

12. Samuel Rodman, Jr., *Diary* (New Bedford, 1927), 261, 293.

13. A court decision of 1783 declared that slavery had no basis in Massachusetts law, and the legislature passed a law forbidding the slave trade in 1788 (Arthur J. Worrall, *Quakers in the Colonial Northeast* [Hanover, N.H., 1980], 156, 164).

14. Lamont D. Thomas, *Rise to Be a People* (Urbana, Ill., 1986), 9, 19.

Bedford Lyceum.[15] The town had once maintained a separate school for black children but by 1838 Douglass observed that "in New Bedford the black man's children—although anti-slavery was far from popular— went to school side by side with the white children and apparently without objection from any quarter."[16]

New Bedford's lack of enthusiasm for the anti-slavery cause, as noted by Douglass, was also commented upon in 1839 by Samuel Rodman, Jr. On December 30 he went to hear George G. Bradburn deliver a lecture on American slavery. The audience was not large, Rodman recorded in his diary, and "The coldness of the ev'g may have been the cause as the abolition zeal of our community is not warm enough to resist a low point in the scale of Farenheit."[17]

Three years later, a meeting of the Bristol County Anti-slavery Society held on August 9, 1842, grew very heated over the issue of the church's role in supporting slavery. When Rodman arrived he found a disorderly rabble at the back of the hall shouting down the speakers. There was shuffling and pushing and finally a general melee as the audience, particularly the women, tried to leave under the protection of the abolitionists. Only one abolitionist was hurt, an unidentified colored man "who was brutally attacked in making his way to the door and rec'd and gave some hard blows."[18]

Within the next decade, the climate in New Bedford began to change. Revulsion against attempted enforcement of the Fugitive Slave Law may have had something to do with it, as well as the regular visits and lectures of eloquent abolitionists like Garrison, Douglass, Charles L. Remond, and Charles C. Burleigh. In 1856 Rodman recorded,

July 29–Aug. 3 . . . On last sixth evening I stopped on my way to mother's at the Town Hall, where I found a large audience listening to the speech of Fred'k Douglass, the negro orator at the close of the public celebration of the First of August, the anniversary of the British emancipation of the slaves in the English Islands of the West Indies. The years that have elapsed since I last heard him

15. Rodman, *Diary*, 224, 269.
16. Frederick Douglass, *My Bondage and My Freedom* (New York, 1855), 347.
17. Rodman, *Diary*, 200.
18. Ibid., 238.

have improved his oratory, the power of which is indicated by the fact that the most quiet and respectful attention was given through his address, which did not end till half past ten o'clock. The scene was in strange contrast with that in our town about twenty years ago when the New England Abolition Society[19] was mobbed and their meeting broken up, though white men of character and talent were the speakers. Here was a meeting called by colored men who alone occupied the platform, with a gratified audience of about a thousand people, a majority of whom were white and more than half women. This speaks favorably for the abatement of prejudice and the advance of humane and just principles.[20]

In that same summer of 1856, a young black man from Troy, New York, came to New Bedford to go on a whaling voyage. Nineteen-year-old James Henry Gooding, called Henry, had not been to sea before. At the Customs House he was issued a seamen's protection paper which would identify him and authorize assistance from United States government representatives should he become stranded in a foreign port. The document recorded that Gooding was of medium height (5′ 5½″), had a brown skin, curly hair, and black eyes. In the offices of the J. & W. R. Wing Company, later to become one of New Bedford's largest whaling firms, his name was entered on the crew list of the firm's new whaleship, the bark *Sunbeam*, with the notations "mulatto" and "green hand."[21]

Gooding's decision to sign on for a whaling voyage reflects the fact that for more than half a century the sea had provided readily available jobs for black men. As a consequence, the proportion of blacks among seafarers was greater than their representation in the general population of the northern states. This was particularly the case in the whaling industry. A survey of the free black population published in 1859 estimated that of 6,000 black men serving in the American merchant marine from Atlantic ports, 2,900 were on board whaleships, where the

19. On Aug. 9, 1842, Rodman had called it a meeting of the Bristol County Anti-slavery Society.

20. Ibid., 330.

21. Customs documents in the records of the New Bedford District Customs House at the New Bedford Free Public Library.

ratio was as high as one man in six.[22] It was certainly true that on some vessels the proportion of black whalemen was even higher. James B. Congdon's father-in-law, Captain Gideon Randall, in a vessel owned by the Quaker Rotch family, once had a crew of thirty in which twenty men were black.[23] There were also a few ships on which everyone including the captain was an African American.

During the early years of the nineteenth century, it was not unusual to encounter black men serving as officers aboard whaleships. The nature of shipboard life—a small, circumscribed community with a rigid hierarchy fixed by rules and duties—placed even the ordinary black seaman on a comparable footing with his white coworkers. By and large, wages were determined by rank, not color, and were generally better than could be earned by blacks elsewhere. The level of integration and fellowship varied from vessel to vessel, but there was usually an easier relationship between the races on shipboard than ashore.[24]

Nevertheless, by the mid-1850s the position of blacks in the whaling fleet, as well as in the maritime industry as a whole, had deteriorated. Writing in 1863, Congdon commented on the fact that most blacks were now signed on as cooks and stewards, "without doubt almost wholly owing to the prejudice of the whites."[25]

For Henry Gooding the position of cook or steward probably offered advantages. As his later writing indicates, he was an intelligent, thoughtful, well-educated young man for whom reading was not just a pastime but a passion. A galley job could mean more time and more privacy both for reading and for the writing that he may have had in mind.

Sunbeam departed New Bedford on July 21, 1856, for a sperm whaling voyage to the Indian and Pacific oceans. The crew included one

---

22. James Freeman Clarke, *Condition of the Free People of Color,* as cited in James B. Farr, "Black Odyssey: The Seafaring Traditions of Afro-Americans" (Ph.D. diss., University of California, Santa Barbara, 1982), 92, 229. Farr suggests that the estimate of black whalemen is probably too high, unless it includes blacks "hired off the African coast."

23. James B. Congdon Papers, Folder 18, "The Colored People of New Bedford," New Bedford Free Public Library.

24. W. Jeffrey Bolster, "To Feel Like a Man: Black Seamen in the Northern States, 1800–1860," *Journal of American History* 76, no. 4 (1990): 1183–85.

25. Congdon Papers, "The Colored People."

other black, sixteen-year-old Albert Seals from Alexandria, Virginia, and three "Kanakas" or Pacific Islanders. Gooding was assigned to the galley early in the voyage, possibly when the cook and fourth mate were off duty with the "venereal."[26] The vessel called at Flores in the Azores, passed the Cape Verde Islands, and headed toward the coast of South America to cruise for whales, then sailed east around the Cape of Good Hope and into the Indian Ocean. On the way, twenty-one-year-old Albert Hooper from Moosehill, Indiana, fell overboard and drowned before a boat could reach him.

After more than three months at sea, *Sunbeam*'s crew took its first whale. In the next four weeks, three more whales were taken and they yielded over 300 barrels of oil. There were the usual small disasters. In February, while taking a large sperm whale, one of the whaleboats was wrecked and *Sunbeam*'s main topgallant yard was carried away when the shipkeepers who had been left behind during the chase tried to tack ship.

Occasionally, the vessel went into port for supplies and the crew was given liberty. At St. Mary's Island near Madagascar, on June 18, 1857, Henry Gooding went on shore with the starboard watch and was reported missing when the rest of the men returned twelve hours later. Gooding's return, which must have occurred, was not recorded in the logbook.

On the world's whaling grounds, encounters with other ships were not infrequent. When the industry was at its height a decade earlier, there were 731 vessels in the American whaling fleet. Even in 1856 the fleet numbered more than 650 whaleships.[27] When a meeting occurred, the two vessels often hove to for a "gam" in which visits, gossip, mail, and reading material were exchanged. At other times the ships simply stopped long enough to "speak" or briefly recount the most important news.

On September 9, 1858, the bark *Sunbeam* was cruising off the western coast of Australia when she "spoke" the bark *Mars* and learned of

26. Logbook of Bark *Sunbeam*, 1856–1859. The Wings' account of the settlement with the crew at the end of the voyage describes Gooding as a "fair cook" (J. & W. R. Wing Accounts for Bark *Sunbeam*, 1856–1859). Both manuscripts at the New Bedford Free Public Library.

27. Alexander Starbuck, *History of the American Whale Fishery from Its Earliest Inception to the Year 1876* (Waltham, 1878; New York, 1964), 688.

the death of Eli Dodge, boatsteerer, whose boat had been stove by a large sperm whale the day before. Dodge was just about Gooding's age and his vessel was also from New Bedford. The two barks had met on several occasions that summer and had even sailed in company for part of the time. It is unlikely that the black cook from Troy became a close friend of the white officer from Hartford, Connecticut. But it is possible that the death of someone who had been in such companionable proximity for a short period of time intensified feelings engendered by the loss of Gooding's own shipmate earlier in the voyage and inspired him to write a poem. Entitled "In Memory of Eli Dodge Who Was Killed by a Whale, Sept. 4, 1858, off the coast of New Holland," the poem is one of six by Gooding that were composed at sea and later printed.[28]

The *Sunbeam* returned to New Bedford on April 13, 1860. When accounts were settled Gooding's share of the net profit, less his debt to the ship, came to $114.42, or about $2.50 per month.[29] This may have been better than average. Elmo P. Hohman, in his classic economic study of the whaling industry, compared the results for three vessels that made a total of twenty-three voyages between 1836 and 1879. Analyzing the settlement accounts of 323 foremast hands, Hohman found that the median cash balance received in one ship was −$11.79, in another it was $000.00 (sic), and in the third $103.20. The median monthly return for seamen in the third vessel was $2.15.[30]

Gooding stayed ashore little more than a month before signing on as steward for a whaling voyage to the eastern Arctic in the bark *Black Eagle*. Apparently there was hope that a new field for right whales was opening up, and ten vessels cleared for Davis Strait and Cumberland Inlet that spring. Gooding's position as steward would give him a higher "lay" or share in the voyage than the green hands or even the seamen.

This was a different kind of whaling altogether, where ice and fog were constant companions and threats, even in midsummer. *Black Eagle*'s owners had elected to have the vessel winter over in Cumber-

---

28. For a further discussion of the poems as well as the poems themselves see Appendix B.

29. Wing accounts for Bark *Sunbeam*.

30. Elmo P. Hohman, *The American Whaleman: A Study of Life and Labor in the Whaling Industry* (New York, 1928), 318.

land Inlet. By December the bark was frozen in and banked with snow for insulation against cold that reached −44° in February. The end of March brought a spell of clear weather and all hands were employed at playing ball for several days when it warmed up to −38°.[31] After another summer in the Arctic, *Black Eagle* returned to New Bedford on November 3, 1861, carrying 1,122 barrels of whale oil and 17,800 pounds of whalebone.[32] The results of the voyage were disappointing. None of the vessels in that fishery returned with a full ship, and the price of oil had already begun to drop in reaction to competition from kerosene, which was derived from the petroleum discovered two years before in Titusville, Pennsylvania. In its "Annual Statement of the Whale Fishery for 1861," the *Whalemen's Shipping List and Merchants' Transcript* wrote that the previous year had been one of unparalled hardship in the industry.[33]

Gooding spent three months on shore and then, abandoning the whaling business, departed in the ship *Richard Mitchell*, a merchant vessel bound for Montevideo to exchange a cargo of general merchandise for wool and hides. On this voyage he was employed as cook and steward at twenty dollars per month, a salary equal to that of the second officer on board.[34] When he returned to New Bedford at the end of the summer, Gooding felt financially secure enough to marry Ellen Louisa Allen, a daughter of Charles and Charlotte Allen of New Bedford. Ellen Allen's father worked as a laborer; her mother was a native of the Azores; Gooding's parents were James and Sarah Gooding, address unknown. The Reverend James D. Butler, chaplain of the Seamen's Bethel, performed the wedding service on September 28, 1862.[35]

31. Logbook of the bark *Black Eagle*, May 20, 1860–Oct. 31, 1861, Kendall Whaling Museum, Sharon, Mass.

32. Starbuck, *History of the American Whale Fishery*, 575.

33. *Whalemen's Shipping List . . .* (New Bedford, 1843–1914), Jan. 7, 1862.

34. Ship *Richard Mitchell* accounts, IMA 365B, microfilm in the Whaling Museum Library of the Old Dartmouth Historical Society. Voyage commenced Jan. 31, 1862.

35. Bristol County, Mass., 1850 Census, as reported in James de T. Abajian, *Blacks in Selected Newspapers, Census, and Other Sources: An Index to Names and Subjects* (Boston, 1977, 1985) 3 vols., 1 suppl. (2 vols.); copy of marriage certificate in Ellen L. Gooding pension records, National Archives, Record Group No. 15, Pension No. WC 21553.

The married couple set up housekeeping at 183 South Water Street just a few blocks from the wharves where Gooding's vessels had tied up. But his maritime career was over. The federal government was about to call upon black men to join in the war to preserve the Union, and when the call came Gooding was ready to respond. On February 14, 1863, just four days after the Fifty-fourth Regiment recruiting office opened on William Street, James Henry Gooding enlisted. He was the eighth person in New Bedford to do so.[36]

At first glance it seems curious that an experienced seaman would choose to join an army regiment rather than enlist in the Union navy. Except for a brief period between 1798 and 1812, the United States Navy had always accepted black seamen in the ranks. The crews were mixed; there were no segregated units. It is true that in 1839 a quota system was introduced that restricted black enlistments each year to 5 percent of the number of white enlistees. That cap had been removed, however, at the beginning of the Civil War. On the other hand there were no black officers and, as in the merchant marine, African Americans tended to occupy the lowest ranks. Thus, for many blacks in the North, it seemed that enlisting in the navy would only perpetuate their second-class citizenship.

There are no precise figures for the number of blacks who enrolled in the Union navy. Some estimates have placed the figure as high as 29,511, or 25 percent of the total force of 118,044 serving in the navy between 1861 and 1865. More recent scholarship, based on an examination of the official rendezvous reports for this period, suggests that only about 9,500 black seamen, or 8 percent of the total, were enrolled, and that about two-thirds of this number were contrabands from the slave states.[37]

The volunteer infantry regiment being organized in Massachusetts during the early months of 1863 seemed to offer an attractive alternative to naval service. Black men were to be enlisted in the special corps

36. List of Volunteers in the 54th Regiment Massachusetts Volunteer Militia [March 1863], Records of the Soldiers' Fund Committee, 1861–1863, New Bedford Free Public Library.

37. David Lawrence Valuska, "The Negro in the Union Navy, 1861–1865" (Ph.D. diss., Lehigh University, 1973), 120–26.

on the same basis and with the same pay as other Massachusetts regiments. At first there was even hope that some of the commissioned officers might be African Americans. Governor Andrew had to give way to the secretary of war on this point, however, and it was not until the end of the war that he was able to arrange for three former sergeants of the regiment to be commissioned and mustered as lieutenants.[38]

A well-disciplined regiment of black soldiers, even without black officers, would be a highly visible example of what African Americans were capable of achieving. To serve the cause of freedom, to prove that they were men of conviction and courage, to suffer alongside their fellow citizens whose skins were white—these were some of the obligations that thoughtful blacks prepared to undertake for the future of their race.

On February 18, a war meeting of colored citizens was held in Liberty Hall, New Bedford. The presiding officer was the Reverend William Jackson, later to become the first black chaplain commissioned in the Union army, and among the vice-presidents was J. H. Gooding. President Jackson reported that nearly half of Captain Grace's company had been raised. He then introduced William Wells Brown from Cambridge. Brown said that blacks had poets and preachers; it was time to have a hero on the battlefield. He knew there were some objections among colored men to enlisting under the present laws that denied them the right to hold commissions, when there were black men as capable as any others to be captain. Nevertheless, he argued, they ought to get over these feelings and realize what progress had been made: they could ride in cars with whites and send their children to integrated schools, and now they were granted the privilege of fighting. The time had come, he concluded, for the black man to vindicate his own character. Other speakers that evening were Colonel Maggi of the Massachusetts Thirty-third Regiment; L. C. Lockwood, in charge of contrabands at Fortress Monroe in Virginia; and Charles L. Remond, the black abolitionist from Salem.[39]

38. The men were Stephen A. Swails, Frank M. Welch, and Peter Vogelsgang (Cornish, *Sable Arm*, 215).
39. New Bedford *Mercury*, Feb. 19, 1863.

William Jackson had been optimistic when he announced at the war meeting that almost half the New Bedford company had already been raised. James B. Congdon, writing to a member of the Boston committee the next day, reported that they had enrolled only thirty men thus far. He went on to say there were 189 eligible black men on New Bedford's rolls, of whom 20 were in other service and 37 abroad, mostly in California, which left only 132 from which to recruit.[40]

The bounties used to encourage the enlistment of white troops were not at first available for blacks. Patriotism and self-interest were supposed to be enough to spur black men to sign up. Many families, however, could ill afford to have a breadwinner go off to war without some kind of assistance to tide them over until the soldier received his pay. Recruiters soon found it necessary to offer financial inducements.

In New Bedford, at the request of Lieutenant Grace, the privately organized Soldiers' Fund Committee distributed ten dollars in February to each of the city's black residents who signed up. Lieutenant Grace also promised bounties of fifty dollars to some men coming from out of state.[41] Later, word reached Congdon that Governor Andrew was opposed to having local communities offer bounties, and a sum authorized by the city's Common Council in early March was hastily designated as aid to needy families instead. The Military Relief Committee, acting on the Council's authorization, voted on March 9, to distribute the sum of twenty-five dollars to each colored citizen, resident of New Bedford, who enlisted in the Fifty-fourth Regiment and was subsequently mustered into the service of the United States.[42]

Governor Andrew, however, wanted all recruits to be enrolled on an equal footing, and viewed any direct payment to an enlisted man as a bounty. Since New Bedford residents were not signing on in numbers to fill a company, there would be inequalities within the final organization that could later sow discontent. Moreover, the state legislature had at last passed a bounty bill to provide fifty dollars for each re-

40. Records of the Soldiers' Fund Committee, 1861–1863, New Bedford Free Public Library.
41. Ibid.; James B. Congdon, Letter to Governor Andrew [photocopy], March 16, 1863, Congdon Papers, "The Colored People."
42. New Bedford *Mercury*, March 10, 1863.

cruit received, accepted, and mustered into United States service. On March 20, therefore, Andrew wrote to the mayor of New Bedford warning that any sum of money distributed to recruits by the city would be deducted from the amount they would receive as a state bounty, "so that no man shall in any case receive, from any source, more than the Fifty Dollars Bounty allowed by the Statute."[43]

With that, the Military Relief Committee abandoned its earlier plans to give money to enlistees and instead advertised for families who were in need to come forward and request aid. The men who had already received ten dollars from the Soldiers' Fund were to return it upon receipt of the state bounty. It is no wonder that Gooding wrote on May 6, "We have heard so many different rumors, about different subjects, that we are rather slow to believe anything we don't see. (Money especially.)" The men were finally mustered for the state bounty on May 14, just two weeks before the regiment left for the field.

The roster of Company C indicates that only thirty-three men, or a good deal less than half the company, were actually from New Bedford.[44] Just as the officers for the regiment had been carefully selected, so also the enlisted men were rigorously screened, and many who signed up were eventually rejected by the examining surgeon on medical grounds. The men had thought to call themselves the Morgan Guards in honor of their local supporter S. Griffitts Morgan, but, declining the honor, Morgan suggested instead the name Toussaint Guards, after the eighteenth-century Haitian patriot.[45]

When the New Bedford group departed for camp on March 4, there were five sergeants on the rolls, including Gooding and William H. Carney, later to win the Medal of Honor for bravery at the battle of Fort Wagner. For some reason, at the time of mustering for the state bounty in May, the men of Company C and of most of the other companies in the regiment were reduced to the rank of private. Noncommissioned officers were subsequently appointed, or reappointed, but Gooding was not promoted to corporal, the highest rank he was to hold, until December 5, 1863.[46]

43. Andrew, Letters Sent, 1861–1865, 13: 458.

44. McKay, "Roster," in Emilio, *History of the Fifty-fourth*, 349–53.

45. New Bedford *Mercury*, March 23, 1863.

46. Descriptive Rolls of the 54th Regiment of the Infantry in the Massachusetts

In his letters, Gooding tells us nothing directly about himself or his military duties. From the official record, we learn only that he served as clerk at the Fourth Brigade headquarters on Morris Island for nine days, from November 6 to 15, 1863.

From a few remarks made by others we learn a bit more. James Congdon described Gooding as "a person of intelligence and cultivation much in advance of a majority of his race."[47] Sergeant Joseph H. Barquet of Company H offered insight into how Gooding's comrades felt about him in two letters that appeared in the *Anglo-African*, a weekly New York newspaper published and edited entirely by blacks. The first, dated Morris Island, January 1864, evidently referred to an article on the pay issue to which Barquet and his friends took exception. "What a stir, Mr. Anglo, you made in our camp!" Barquet wrote. "Had a shell from the bushwackers fell in the Quartermaster's big tent, the stir could not have been greater. 'Hand it in here.' 'Hand what?' 'That paper.' 'No, let Barquet'—'No, let the immortal Gooding read. . . .'"[48]

One week after Barquet's letter was published, Gooding was wounded in the thigh at Olustee, Florida, and was taken prisoner. For the next five months he suffered the horrors of Andersonville Prison, where he died on July 19, 1864. Writing of the battle some years later, William Wells Brown said, "Colonel Hallowell ordered the color-line to be advanced one hundred and fifty paces. Three of the colored corporals, Pease, Palmer and Glasgow being wounded, and the accomplished Goodin[g] killed, there were four only left, . . ."[49]

All three men who wrote of Gooding, one white and two black, recognized that he was someone with exceptional talent. Sergeant Barquet mentioned him again in "A Soldier's Letter to the National Convention," saying:

Volunteers, Under the Command of Colonel Robert G. Shaw, [corrected on the thirteenth and fourteenth days of May]; also Muster-out Roll, Company C, Commonwealth of Massachusetts Military Division History Research and Museum, Natick.

47. Congdon's notation follows extract from Gooding letter dated July 20, 1863, in Congdon Papers, Folder 6a, New Bedford Free Public Library.

48. *Anglo-African*, Feb. 13, 1864. I am grateful to Edwin S. Redkey of the State University of New York at Purchase for sharing copies of the Barquet letters with me.

49. William Wells Brown, *The Negro in the American Rebellion* (Boston, 1867), 222. At first, Gooding was reported killed and in April 1864 his widow applied for a pension. Official notification of his death at Andersonville was not received until May 22, 1865.

I know you will not fail to notice our doings, or the part we are acting in this sublimely terrible drama, forgetting not that in our hands the honor, safety, and future of our people's welfare lie— that the walls of prejudice has fallen before the blast of our con- duct—that voluntarily the witnesses take the stand, and Port Hudson, Wagner, Olustee, Petersburg, Fort Pillow, Milliken's Bend, becomes the starting of our military history, without recall- ing Red Bank, Erie, New Orleans; that Small, Rivers, Morris, Kearney, Tilmon sign the roll of fame with Attucks, Van Bracklen, and Harcourt—that Wilson, Swails, Wilkins, Gooding, Lennox, Peel are the names that will never die with us. . . .[50]

Intelligent, cultivated, accomplished, even immortal—these were words used to describe Gooding by his contemporaries. Yet there is no documentary evidence so far discovered to indicate precisely where and how Gooding was educated or how he spent the first nineteen years of his life before turning up in New Bedford in July 1856. Both his sea- men's protection paper and his marriage certificate say that he was born in Troy, New York, yet there is no record of the Gooding family there, either in census reports or in city directories, from 1827 to 1863.

Gooding's father may have been a laborer on the railroads, or the canals, or both, in upper New York state. One of the letters describes a shot from a Brooke's gun as a "noise . . . like an Erie lightening-express train." Later in the same letter, Gooding comments on the difficulties of building Fort Wagner and Battery Gregg under a constant rain of rebel shells saying, "it takes about as much courage to hold them as it did to take them, and then to work on them and completely change them is something more than digging on a canal or railroad."

Troy served as a port of departure for points west and north on the

50. *Anglo-African*, Nov. 5, 1864. Barquet's list of battles in which African Americans played heroic roles, and the list of black heroes, includes the names of five men from the 54th in addition to Gooding. Pvt. George Wilson of Co. A earned distinguished merit at the battle of Fort Wagner; Sgt. Stephen A. Swails of Co. F was commissioned a lieutenant after serving with distinction until the war's end; Sgt. James H. Wilkins of Co. D bore the national flag at Olustee; Sgt. Charles W. Lennox of Co. A bore the national flag in the attack on James Island; and Corp. Henry F. Peal of Co. F carried the state colors at Olustee until he was mortally wounded, when he handed them on to Corp. Preston Helman of Co. E.

Erie and Champlain canals, and one of their many branches went to Seneca, New York, where a James Goodin (no g) was recorded in the state census of 1850.[51] Then too, various sections of railroad between Albany and Buffalo, which were consolidated to form the New York Central in 1853, were under construction in the years of Gooding's childhood and early teens. It is also possible that Gooding himself worked as a laborer before going to sea.

Henry Gooding's education, whether it took place in a formal setting or was self-directed, was exceptional. It is obvious from the letters published in the New Bedford *Mercury* that he had read widely in literature, history, and the classics and that he had a strong social conscience. If indeed he did grow up in Troy, Gooding would have been part of a lively black community committed to the abolition of slavery, to education, and to the political and social advancement of the race. In 1841, when he was about four years old, the first Negro State Convention was held there, and from that grew the National Convention of Colored People and later the NAACP. There were several schools for black children in Troy, one of which was taught for a time by Henry Highland Garnet, later the first minister of the first black church in that city.[52] If Gooding's father moved about a great deal, the child may have lived with his mother's family in Troy and attended school there.[53]

Gooding's relationship with the New Bedford *Mercury* is yet another unexplained facet of his life. In the year between March 3, 1863, and February 22, 1864, the newspaper published one of his letters almost every week. It seems probable that the arrangements were made before Gooding left New Bedford; perhaps after leaving the sea he had found employment there.

Founded in 1807, the *Mercury* had a venerable history, although it had not always held abolitionist sentiments. After the tumultuous

51. The New York State Census lists a James Gooding at Bristol in 1830, at Barre in 1840, and at Otsego in 1850, as well as a Sarah Gooding at Cortland in 1850. I am grateful to Robert N. Andersen of the Rensselaer County Historical Society for searching city directories and for supplying information about the black community in Troy, and to Robert B. Hudson of the Troy Public Library for reviewing census reports.

52. Samuel Rezneck, *Profiles Out of the Past of Troy, N.Y. since 1789* (Troy, N.Y., 1970), 119–22.

53. This is pure speculation. The maiden name of Gooding's mother is not known.

meeting of the Bristol County Anti-slavery Society in 1842, Samuel Rodman cancelled his subscription to the newspaper, saying, "Today I ordered the 'Mercury,' which I have taken from the commencement of my house keeping, discontinued on account of its anti-abolition bias as indicated by its silence on the exciting occurrences of last week, and reference to them today in a sneer. . . ."[54]

The newspaper was purchased in 1861 by C. B. H. Fessenden and William G. Baker. The new owners supported the Republican administration in its prosecution of the war. The *Mercury* was one of the earliest newspapers to advocate the arming of enslaved negroes ("We must fight them or free them"),[55] and from the outset it took an interest in the Fifty-fourth Regiment, which was reflected both in its editorials and in its news coverage. On May 11, 1863, the editors described a visit they had made to Camp Meigs on the previous Saturday, when they were taken around by Sergeant Gooding and Corporal Delavan of Company C to inspect the barracks, cooking quarters, and quartermaster's department. They were impressed with the neatness of the grounds, the cleanliness of the barracks, and the "moral worth" of the men.[56] One can imagine that they also may have made arrangements with Gooding to continue his reports after the regiment left for the field.

Gooding's letters, when published, were given a prominent position at or near the top of an inside page of the newspaper. Almost invariably they were headed {Correspondence of the Mercury}/Letter from the 54th (Colored) Regiment, followed by the place and date. For the first six months the letters were signed with Gooding's initials—J. H. G. Then, on August 5, the *Mercury*'s editors identified their correspondent as a member of Company C of the Fifty-fourth Massachusetts Regiment. Shortly afterward Gooding began to use the pseudonym "Monitor," no doubt in response to recent general orders that prohibited giving military information to friends or to the public press.[57]

The *Mercury*'s note had also described Gooding as "a truthful and

---

54. Rodman, *Diary*, 238 (Aug. 15, 1842).
55. Ellis, *History of New Bedford*, 530.
56. New Bedford *Mercury*, May 11, 1863.
57. General Orders, No. 66, issued Aug. 7, 1863.

intelligent correspondent, and a good soldier." Curiously, the editors made no comment when they published a letter from Captain Grace on March 9, 1864, announcing (incorrectly, as it turned out), that Gooding had been killed during the battle at Olustee in late February. Perhaps they felt it was enough to have given his talent a voice during his lifetime. Certainly for me, it has been a privilege to help in making that voice heard once again.

Acknowledgments

The poems and letters of James Henry Gooding were rediscovered through a series of happy accidents. Two years ago, in going through some odds and ends to be cataloged for the Old Dartmouth Historical Society's Whaling Museum Library, I came across the six broadside poems. The one about Eli Dodge led me to crew lists from the New Bedford customs records, and then to the discovery that Gooding was a mulatto. Frustrated at being unable to find out anything more about the publication history of the poems or about other writing that Gooding might have done, I turned to Carl Cruz, a descendant of Sergeant Carney, who has been collecting information about New Bedford's black community for some time. Cruz gave me an article written by Everett Allen, which discussed a letter sent to President Abraham Lincoln by a black soldier in the Massachusetts Fifty-fourth Regiment.[58] The article was about Gooding and included a transcript of his letter to Lincoln, as well as facsimiles of documents from his military file in the National Archives.[59] Later, Allen arranged to have his research notes about Gooding sent to me. Unfortunately, he had been unable to find out anything about Gooding's early life. Gooding's marriage had been childless and there were no direct descendants; surviving members of Ellen Gooding's family knew little except that her husband had been a seaman and had died in the Civil War.

One day I walked up to the New Bedford Free Public Library to have a look at the James Congdon Papers there, on a hunch that this might

58. Everett S. Allen, "A Letter to President Lincoln," [New Bedford] *Sunday Standard-Times*, Feb. 20, 1972.

59. Gooding's letter to Lincoln is included in Appendix A.

somehow lead to further information. There were two fat files containing extracts of articles about the Civil War that Congdon had copied from the *Mercury*. As I flipped through the pages trying to decipher Congdon's almost illegible handwriting, it struck me that several of the extracts were followed by the initials J. H. G. I began paying more attention, and eventually came to a paragraph after which Congdon had written in full, "James Henry Gooding," and then in brackets, "Gooding was a New Bedford man, and as will be seen by his letter a person of intelligence and cultivation much in advance of a majority of his race. He was taken prisoner afterwards and died in a rebel prison July 19, 1864. J. B. C."[60] Eureka! These letters published in the *Mercury* revealed an aspect of Gooding as unrecognized as the poems, and potentially much more interesting.

Altogether, forty-eight letters have been located and transcribed. The generosity of Paul Cyr and the New Bedford Free Public Library allowed me to make copies of Gooding's letters from a microfilm of the *Mercury*, and the kindness of my husband, Thomas R. Adams, who gave me access to his computer terminal, enabled me to spend long winter evenings transcribing them.

The letters have been copied almost exactly as to spelling, punctuation, and paragraphing. Obvious typographical slips, such as ctiy for city, and a handful (less than ten) misspellings have been corrected; awkwardly placed commas have been deleted; and words or letters apparently left out inadvertently have been added in brackets. I have also standardized the punctuation of the datelines and signatures.

Explanatory notes were derived from a variety of sources but I referred often to Luis F. Emilio's *A Brave Black Regiment*, which is the most complete and detailed account of the Fifty-fourth to date. Emilio was sixteen when war broke out. He enlisted October 19, 1861, and was on active service until March 1865. For two of those years he served as captain of Company E of the Fifty-fourth. Twenty-five years later Emilio assembled material to write a regimental history. In a series of chronologically arranged scrapbooks now at the Massachusetts Historical Society, he compiled documents that included his own letters and daily record of events, contemporary diaries and recollec-

60. See n. 47 above.

tions solicited from fellow officers, photographs, newspaper clippings, and a variety of ephemera, and then he wrote the history of the regiment. Wherever it seemed appropriate I have compared or augmented Gooding's account of an event with Emilio's.

Sidney Kaplan recognized at once the importance of Gooding's letters and brought them to the attention of the University of Massachusetts Press. Professor Kaplan also gave valuable encouragement and advice in the early stages of my research.

Others who have been particularly helpful include Georgia B. Barnhill, American Antiquarian Society; Floyd A. Scott, Andersonville National Historic Site; J. Rufus Fears, Boston University; Alan Boegehold, Brown University; Peter Harrington and Jennifer Lee, John Hay Library, Brown University; Cynthia D. Bond and Henry Louis Gates, Cornell University; the Reverend Eugene V. N. Goetchius, Cummaquid; Russell Duncan, John Carroll University; Joost Schokkenbroek, Kendall Whaling Museum; Peter Drummey, Brenda Lawson, and Virginia H. Smith, Massachusetts Historical Society; Dana Essigman and James E. Fahey, Commonwealth of Massachusetts Military Division History Research and Museum; William Mulhomme, Massachusetts Archives at Columbia Point; Philip Weimerskirch, Providence Public Library; Richard C. Kugler, Old Dartmouth Historical Society; Robert N. Andersen, Rensselaer County Historical Society; Kenneth Rivard, Somerville; Edwin S. Redkey, State University of New York at Purchase; Robert B. Hudson, Troy Public Library; Edwin Gittleman, University of Massachusetts at Boston; Laurie Kahn-Leavitt, WGBH; and Martha Matzke, Yale University.

I am grateful to all those who shared their knowledge and their time so generously.

On the Altar of Freedom

1

Looking Quite Like Soldiers
Massachusetts, March through May 1863

On March 4 at 2 P.M. the New Bedford company for the Fifty-fourth assembled at City Hall, where roll was called and James B. Congdon offered a few remarks. Each man was then given a pair of mittens. Following the ceremonies the group marched to the railroad depot escorted by a band and a crowd of well-wishers. Three more men joined there, making a total of fifty-four recruits who departed for Camp Meigs.[1]

The training camp at Readville was in a flat open area a few miles southwest of Boston. Here the men were housed in large wooden barracks, which could double as drilling grounds in snowy or wet weather. The welfare of all the regiments in camp was nominally the responsibility of the commandant, Brigadier General Richard A. Pierce.

[*Mercury*, March 3, 1863]

Messrs. Editors:—As the time draws near for the departure of the men Capt. Grace[2] has recruited, for camp, and there is not a sufficient

1. New Bedford *Mercury*, March 5, 1863.

2. Grace had hoped for a commission as captain, and he was often referred to as such until the New Bedford contingent arrived at Camp Meigs. Despite lobbying by leading citizens of the city, however, Colonel Shaw declined to recommend him for a captaincy. (Massachusetts Archives, at Columbia Point, Executive Department Letters, 1862–

number to form a whole company, does it not behoove every colored man in this city to consider, rationally with himself, whether he cannot be one of the glorious 54th? Are the colored men here in New Bedford, who have the advantage of education, so blind to their own interest, in regard to their social development, that through fear of some double dealing, they will not now embrace probably the only opportunity that will ever be offered them to make themselves a people. There are a great many I must confess, who, Micawber-like, "are waiting for something to turn up"; but they will have to learn sooner or later, that if anything does "turn up" to their advantage, they will have to be the means of turning it up themselves; they must learn that there is more dignity in carrying a musket in defence of liberty and right than there is in shaving a man's face, or waiting on somebody's table.—Not that it is any degradation to perform those offices, but those who perform them are considered nothing but appendages to society; for in either case, the recipients of these favors could perform them for themselves on a "pinch."

Another class are those who argue "it won't pay to go for a soger"; but I think there are not nine out of ten who will realize as much in a year here at home as a man will in the army in the same length of time. And again, if the colored man proves to be as good a soldier as it is confidently expected he will, there is a permanent field of employment opened to him, with all the chances of promotion in his favor. Such an event is not unlikely in this country, any more than it is in India and other colonial dependencies of England. In India the native militia is considered equal if not superior to the English soldiery in tactics and bravery, and there are natives holding the highest military positions. Our people must know that if they are ever to attain to any position in the eyes of the civilized world, they must forego comfort, home, fear, and above all, superstition, and fight for it; make up their minds to become something more than hewers of wood and drawers of water all their lives. Consider that on this continent, at least, their race and name will be totally obliterated unless they put forth some effort now to save themselves.

G.—One of the 54th

1863, vol. 21b, no. 55, 56). Grace was promoted to the higher rank on July 19, 1863, after the battle of Fort Wagner.

[*Mercury*, March 7, 1863]

Camp Meigs, Readville, March 6

Messrs. Editors:—Immediately upon our arrival here on Wednesday afternoon, we marched to the barracks, where we found a nice warm fire and a good supper in readiness for us. During the evening the men were all supplied with uniforms, and now they are looking quite like soldiers. They all seem contented, and appear in the best spirits. We have drill morning and afternoon, and the men are taking hold with a great degree of earnestness.

Col. Shaw is on the ground, doing all he can for the comfort of those now in camp. Lieut. Dexter has been appointed to the New Bedford company, but has not yet made his appearance.[3]

The men from New Bedford are the largest in camp and it is desired to fill up the company from our city, which can and ought to be done. Lieut. Grace will be in the city tomorrow and he wants to bring a squad back with him.

[Unsigned]

[*Mercury*, March 18, 1863]

Camp Meigs, Readville, March 15

Messrs. Editors:—Presuming a few lines from this locality would prove interesting to some of your many readers, I have taken upon myself the task of penning them. Among the men in this camp the New Bedford men stand A No. 1, in military bearing, cleanliness and morality; not because I happen to belong to the New Bedford company do I assert this, for if the other companies proved to be better ordered than ours, I should be proud to confirm it. All the men appear to regard Capt. Grace with (I might say) veneration; for he presents that un-

3. Col. Robert Gould Shaw, who would command the regiment, was then twenty-five years old. He enlisted at the beginning of the war, fought at Cedar Mountain and Antietam, and most recently had been a captain in the 2d Massachusetts Infantry. Second Lt. Benjamin Franklin Dexter, a forty-three-year-old printer from Cambridge, Mass., had also enlisted in April 1861 and had served three tours of duty in various Massachusetts regiments before joining Company C of the 54th.

common combination of a man strict in military discipline, but always tempered with kindness; a man who will go to the utmost length of his military power to assist or benefit an inferior. A better man, in my judgment, could not have been placed in command of a company of colored men; for he seems to have studied the peculiar modes of thought, action and disposition of the colored men so well, that there is the most cheerful obedience rendered to the most imperative command. These opinions are not hastily formed, but are arrived at by a close and careful observation of things as they are.

We have prayers every morning and evening, most of the men taking part in them; and I need not add that there is a great degree of fervor exhibited vide Bethel Church, Kempton street.[4] As for myself I find it somewhat dull when I am not on duty, as I have nothing to read, although it is a source of amusement to watch some of the odd capers or listen to some of the equally ludicrous speeches, so peculiar to some of our class of people. They are all anxious to perfect themselves in drill that they may the sooner meet the Rebs, and they all feel determined to fight; they all say that is their wish, and I cannot doubt it, for there seems to be a sort of preternatural earnestness about their expressions which no one can mistake. They do not, some of them, yet exactly comprehend the future benefits of enlisting, but they have an impulse equally as great, so far as they are capable of understanding it, and that is revenge. Hoping the Relief Committee[5] have paid the money to the families of those who are here in camp, for I know some who needed it very much, I will close.

J. H. G.

[*Mercury*, March 24, 1863]

Camp Meigs, Readville, March 21

Messrs. Editors:—The glorious 54th (that is to be) is getting on nicely, there being now in camp 368 men, two companies, A and B,

---

4. The African [Methodist Episcopal] Bethel Church on Kempton Street, New Bedford, was first organized in 1842. Although not the earliest black church in New Bedford (the African Christian Church was established there in 1826), it was the first to have a denominational tie with churches elsewhere. William Grimes, appointed a chaplain at Camp Meigs, was pastor there in 1863.

5. The New Bedford Military Relief Committee.

being full, and C and D wanting a few more men to fill them up, which can easily be done in a very few days. We have five men in our company who are enlisted, but expect them to be discharged, on account of physical disability; indeed, if every man had been received who applied, I think it would very near have filled five companies.

The men appear to be all very well satisfied, except a few in Cos. A and B, who are of a class to be satisfied with nothing. Two of them attempted to skedaddle last Friday night, but were brought to by feeling a bayonet in the rear, as Co. C had sentinels posted at the time. They say their grounds for trying to desert are that they have received no bounty, as was represented they should as soon as they had enlisted and been sworn in. I think the men who are about the country recruiting should not misrepresent the conditions, but leave it more to the judgment and patriotism of men to enlist, simply providing conveyance to the camp, as, I think, they are authorized to do. As regards the men who came from New Bedford in this company, they do not seem to think so much about any bounty, but, by the vote of the City Council, a sum of money was appropriated for the relief of the families of colored citizens enlisted in the 54th regiment, and some of the men fear their families are suffering now for the want of their customary support.

You, Messrs. Editors, may be well aware that colored men generally, as a class, have nothing to depend upon but their daily labor; so, consequently, when they leave their labors and take up arms in defence of their country, their homes are left destitute of those little necessities which their families must enjoy as well as those of white men; and as the city has passed a resolution to pay them a sum, they would rather their families received it than become objects of public charity. We are all determined to act like men, and fight, money or not; but we think duty to our families will be a sufficient excuse for adverting to the subject.

John H. Atkinson, of New Bedford, is in the hospital, very sick.[6] I could not ascertain exactly what his complaint is, but think it is the effect of cold. With that exception the health of the men is very good. We have a very pleasant time in our barracks every evening, having music, singing, and sometimes dancing. We have two musicians who

---

6. Atkinson's name does not appear in George F. McKay's "Roster of the Fifty-fourth Massachusetts Infantry," in Emilio, *History of the Fifty-fourth*, 327–92.

regale us with very fine music—a great deal better than a 'feller' pays to hear sometimes.

The ladies of the Relief Society will please accept the thanks of Co. C. for those shirts, socks and handkerchiefs, which should have been expressed in the last letter. God bless the ladies.[7]

J. H. G.

P.S. Wm. T. Boyd, of Pa., died this day (23d). He was in the hospital but two days. He was a member of Co. B.

J. H. G.

[*Mercury*, March 31, 1863]

Camp Meigs, Readville, March 30

Messrs. Editors:—As the week begins anew, I have condensed my notes of the past week to lay them before the readers of the Mercury. In my last I stated the number of men in camp to be 368; today the number is 439, an increase of 71 men in one week, one more company having been organized, making five companies. During the past week things have assumed a more military shape than ever before, owing to the fine state of the weather, permitting out-door drilling. Since the men have been in camp the drilling has been conducted in empty barracks, until the past week. It is quite enlivening to see squads of men in the open field, a little distance from the barracks, going through their evolutions; especially when they acquit themselves so creditably as the officers say they do. And here I may remark that every officer in camp appears to take an interest in the speedy and correct discipline of the men; neither are they lacking in regard for the religious welfare of the men, receiving the proffers of religious men willingly, who desire to make any remarks beneficial to the men. Rev. Wm. Jackson is here, and is to act as chaplain pro tem.[8] Mr. Rickers, City Missionary, from Boston, preached yesterday forenoon, and Rev. Mr. Jackson in the afternoon.

7. The New Bedford Ladies' Soldiers' Relief Society was organized in mid-April 1861, after the departure of the city's first volunteer infantrymen, to provide necessities like clothing and hospital stores, as well as treats, for the men.

8. Pastor of the Salem Baptist Church in New Bedford, Jackson was appointed a post chaplain at Camp Meigs on March 23. In mid-July he became chaplain of the 55th

I see a rumor in the Boston Herald that the conscription act will be put in force by taking the Northern colored people first. If it be true, the young, able bodied colored men of New Bedford would do well to come up here to Readville, "out of the cold." The New York World thinks Gov. Andrew is exasperated because the colored people won't enlist. There may be more truth than sarcasm in the hint.[9]

The Editors of the MERCURY will please accept the thanks of Company C, for a bundle of magazines, and serials. Also, some unknown friends, for towels, looking glasses, blacking and brushes, and three barrels of apples. These acts of kindness make us all feel that we are not forgotten by the good people of New Bedford. If those we left behind fare in proportion as well as we do, we are content.

J. H. G.

[*Mercury*, April 6, 1863]

Camp Meigs, Readville, April 3

Messrs. Editors:—The 54th progresses daily. This week past the men who have been in camp the longest time have been practicing in the manual of arms. It really makes one's heart pulsate with pride as he looks upon those stout and brawny men, fully equipped with Uncle Sam's accoutrements upon them, to feel that these noble men are practically refuting the base assertions reiterated by copperheads[10] and traitors that the black race are incapable of patriotism, valor or ambition. Officers of distinction, whose judgements are not warped by prejudice, pronounce this regiment to be the nucleus of an army equaling in

Massachusetts Regiment, apparently the first black chaplain ever to receive an official commission from the U.S. government (Edwin S. Redkey, "Black Chaplains in the Union Army," *Civil War History* 32, no. 4 [1987]: 332).

9. Thus far, after almost two months of recruiting, only 439 men, less than half a regiment, had signed up. The Enrollment Act of 1863, passed by Congress on March 3, was designed to stimulate volunteering by threatening a draft if regional quotas were not filled within fifty days of a draft call. The first call under this act was not issued until July 1863 (New Bedford *Mercury*, March 30, 1863; McPherson, *Battle Cry of Freedom*, 601).

10. Also known as Peace Democrats, Copperheads were opposed to President Lincoln's war policy and sought to restore the union through negotiation. They were also anti-black, anti-abolitionist, and pro-slavery.

discipline and material the Imperial Hosts of Europe. I, for one, hope their liberal assumptions will in the end prove true—and it is merely a question of time to make it so. Our first dress parade took place this afternoon, and those who know say the men behaved admirably, for so short a period in drilling.

Last Monday all the organized companies on the ground were mustered in the State service; after this was consummated, some of the "boys" in Co. B became a little clamorous for their "bounty"; in fact, it seemed as though they were inclined to be "muzzy,"[11] but a slight intimation from the Colonel about the "guard house," wearing patent bracelets, and sundry other terrors in store for pugnacious gentlemen, under Uncle Sam's tuition, tended to quiet them wonderfully. They appear to have forgotten all about their grievances, in the emulation of the other companies in drilling—which I think is very good. The sanitary condition of the men is very good, considering the location of the camp, it being situated in a valley, and consequently very damp. During the wet weather we had last month, colds and coughs were very prevalent among the men; but now those complaints are most wholly ended, owing no doubt to the improvement in the weather, and becoming accustomed to the locality.

Rev. Wm. Jackson has been laboring very faithfully the past week among us, but the fruits of his labor are yet to be tested. I hope they will prove successful, and I have no doubt in some instances they will.

The number of men in camp is 459; there is a barrack being fitted up now, which is, I presume, for the reception of expected recruits. Tell the young men in New Bedford there is an ample chance for them to get in the 54th yet; not to hang back because there is no recruiting office open in the city; but come "right up to the scratch"; don't let the boys who *are* here get all the honor, but come, and we will share it with them.

J. H. G.

April 4th. This morning we have an addition of 40 men. They came into camp with colors flying, and were received with three hearty cheers. This makes our number 499 men, a half regiment lacking a few men.

J. H. G.

11. Muddled or confused of mind; stupefied as with liquor.

[*Mercury*, April 13, 1863]

Camp Meigs, Readville, April 11

Messrs. Editors.—Since my last weekly epistle, we have received 315 recruits, making the total number 614, and more expected daily. The ground about the barracks has dried enough now to make walking quite a pleasure. Our company have been presented with a couple of foot-balls by Lieut. Grace, and they are a source of amusement and recreation to the whole regiment. The regiment attracts considerable attention, if judged by the number of visitors we have, including a goodly portion of ladies.

Rev. Wm. Jackson desires to say through the MERCURY, in order to clear up some false impressions which have obtained, through the Pastor of the A.M.E. Church, that he did NOT apply, either in person or by letter to the governor, for the chaplaincy of the 54th; that the appointment was made at the suggestion of some friends of his in Boston; furthermore, it was unnecessary for the Pastor of the "Bethel Church" to publish his resignation when he never held any position to resign. Mr. Jackson has in his possession a letter from Secretary Hayden,[12] which will substantiate the above statement. I think myself, Mr. Jackson has been the victim of prejudice—all we want for him is fair play.[13]

---

12. Lewis Hayden had been born a slave in Kentucky. He escaped, eventually bought his freedom, and came to Boston about 1850. A leader of his race and a friend of John Andrew, Hayden took an active part in organizing the 54th.

13. On March 23, 1863, by special order of Governor Andrew, Rev. William Grimes and Rev. William Jackson were appointed to act alternately as chaplains of the post at Readville. Grimes declined, saying that although he could fill in for Jackson at his church, Jackson would not be acceptable to the Bethel Church congregation. Under the circumstances, Grimes would have to resign his pastorate to accept the part-time position. This he would be glad to do if a future appointment as full-time chaplain to the 54th Regiment could be assured. Such assurances were evidently not made. Jackson served as post chaplain until July 14, 1863, when he was named regimental chaplain in the Massachusetts 55th (Colored) Regiment. The 54th was apparently without a regimental chaplain until the Rev. Samuel Harrison of Pittsfield, Mass., was commissioned on Sept. 8, 1863 (Andrew, Letters Sent, 1861–1865, 13: 527; William Grimes, Letter to General R. A. Pierce in Records of Camp Meigs, Richard A. Pierce Papers, New Bedford Free Public

The camp was visited yesterday by Surgeon General Dale,[14] who expressed himself well satisfied with [the] physical appearance of the men. Surgeon Stone, acting in this regiment, had all the men vaccinated yesterday, as a preventive against small pox.[15] There is not much sickness in camp, considering the number of men present, there being but three men unable to walk out of doors. The men are growing fat, rugged, but not saucy.

Tell the ladies that our boys think there are no women anywhere so good as the New Bedford ladies; and one, who belongs to our company but not to New Bedford, said, "I guess them New Bedford wimmin must be mighty good lookin'" "Why so?" says one. "Cause they are allers sendin' us somethin'." After that speech the boys gave three cheers for the ladies of the Relief Society, expressive of thanks for sewing purses containing needles, thread, buttons, yarn, a thimble and paper of pins, one for each man.

J. H. G.

[*Mercury*, April 21, 1863]

Camp Meigs, Readville, April 18

Messrs. Editors:—The past week has been marked by nothing extraordinary with us here, excepting a share of fine weather, which must be considered out of the "common order of things" compared with the mud and mire experienced all spring. The total number of men in camp is now 674, making an increase of 60 men for the week; but they do not come fast enough for the boys who are here. We want to get the regiment full, and show that we are men. Certainly there are some here who would be as well suited if they were away, and the majority of the men would be very glad if they were drummed out. They differ none

---

Library; Charles Bernard Fox, *Record of the Service of the Fifty-fifth Massachusetts Volunteer Infantry* [Cambridge, 1868], 101; McKay, "Roster," in Emilio, *History of the Fifty-fourth*, 331).

14. William J. Dale, surgeon-general of Massachusetts.

15. Lincoln R. Stone accompanied the regiment to the South and was present during the assault on Fort Wagner. At the end of 1863 he was appointed Surgeon, U.S. Volunteers.

though, in that respect, from other regiments. So long as patriotism was made a purchaseable article there were plenty of men to fill the ranks, but now, when it is not a "paying concern" nobody cares much about going. But *our* people must consider that their position is a very delicate one; the least false step, at a moment like the present, may tell a dismal tale at some future day. Let them consider that a chance to obtain what they have "spouted" for in "convention assembled" now presents itself by works, not by words! And let them remember that the Greeks lost their liberties by "too much talk"; thinking that talking would accomplish more than fighting; but they saw their mistake when it was too late.[16] Let our people beware. Their fate will be worse than that of the Greeks, if they do not put forth an effort now to save themselves. As one of the race, I beseech you not to trust to a fancied security, laying comfort to your minds, that our condition will be bettered, because slavery must die. It depends on the free black men of the North, whether it will die or not—those who are in bonds must have some one to open the door; when the slave sees the white soldier approach, he dares not trust him and why? because he has heard that some have treated him worse than their owners in rebellion. But if the slave sees a black soldier, he knows he has got a friend; and through friendship, he that was once a slave can be made a soldier, to fight for his own liberty. But allow that slavery will die without the aid of our race to kill it—language cannot depict the indignity, the scorn, and perhaps violence, that will be heaped upon us; unthought of laws will be enacted, and put in force, to banish us from the land of our birth; and European governments, who now dare not recognize the Southern Confederacy, will call the ostracism a just measure. Now is the time to act,—emulate the men of Pennsylvania, who have left their homes in numbers to shame the colored men of the "Old Bay State," the "Cradle of Liberty." This regiment should be filled now, with what is wanted to fill it, 326 more men, from Massachusetts; and if our people will only take hold of

16. Plutarch recorded that the statesman Phocion once said to the Athenians, "My good people, stick to the weapons you know how to use; talk, don't fight." Fourth-century Greeks, threatened with the increasing power of Philip of Macedonia, could not rouse themselves to unite for action until too late and were defeated at Chaeronea in August 338 B.C. (M. A. Hamilton, *Greece* [Oxford, 1926], 210, 212).

the matter in earnest it can be done. Let the young women drive all those young loungers off to the war, and if they won't go, say "I'm no more gal of thine." There are a plenty of young men in Boston, New Bedford, and other smaller places in the State to fill this regiment up in a very short time. We want them to feel as though they must go, not go purposely for a bounty, but go for honor, duty and liberty.[17]

We were beautifully sold[18] last Wednesday. It was rumored about the Camp that Governor Andrew was to visit the Camp; so the boys all thought of course they must have everything in apple-pie order; we had the barracks all cleaned and hung with holly, and everything looked splendidly. But it turned out that some of the companies wanted to prove which was the smartest.

J. H. G.

[*Mercury,* April 27, 1863]

Camp Meigs, Readville, April 25

Messrs. Editors:—The past week's report of the 54th is encouraging, if not stirring. The number of recruits for the past week is 66 making a total of 740 men. Indeed, to see the men on dress parade, one would think there was a full regiment, when there is not more than 630, the balance being required for guard or fatigue duties. The most of the companies are now quite proficient in the manual of arms, and perform

---

17. Philadelphia, with a black population over five times that of Boston and New Bedford combined, was the headquarters of a vigorous recruitment effort and sent more than 100 enlistees to the Massachusetts 54th Regiment in February and March 1863. Over half were enrolled in Company B. On February 26 the New Bedford *Mercury* defended its city's black community. "One word more in relation to the small number of recruits for the colored regiment in New Bedford. The office was opened less than a fortnight since. There are in our city 132 colored men enrolled as liable to do military duty. In this short space and out of this handful of men FORTY SEVEN have enrolled their names. What town in Massachusetts has contributed as large a proportion of its arms-bearing population and raised them so expeditiously?" (Data relating to Philadelphia recruits extracted from McKay, "Roster," in Emilio, *History of the Fifty-fourth,* 327–91).

18. Tricked.

the evolutions with as much precision as a great many older troops. Soldiers and officers from other camps say they never thought it possible for men to learn in so short a time as much as these men have. The camp was visited by several members of the Legislature the past week, who expressed themselves highly pleased with the efficiency, discipline and cleanliness of the men; and one gentleman paid us a compliment by saying our barracks looked neater than those on the other side of the railroad. But the praise for that is due to Col. Shaw, whose quick eye detects anything in a moment out of keeping with order or military discipline. It is the best way to begin, saving a deal of trouble in the end; without order, the best men on earth would be worthless for military purposes.

Rev. Mr. Jackson is still with us, laboring for the soles, if the uppers are neglected—because there are men in this regiment who forget that there are other combs besides Combe on the understanding.[19] Now Messrs. Editors, we want some more New Bedford men; if they don't make up their minds very soon, the gate will be shut; every week the number wanted becomes less, and will our New Bedford men see those from other States earning their right to manhood? Where are all the loud orators, whose patriotic appeals said go to the war, we are with you? Come out, ye brave men, we want to see ye. And where, oh! where are the leaders of men? Why don't they send one representative to the war? so they can say, "We filled our quota." Don't let the Journal of Commerce, and other powerful organs, have a chance to tell the truth about you, when they say "The colored man don't know what's good for him." Rise up from your lethargy, and prove by your works that they know not what they say, or else—go and bag your heads.

J. H. G.

19. Gooding seems to have tripped on the intricacies of his double play on words and substituted the nineteenth-century British phrenologist and educator George Combe, author of *The Constitution of Man Considered in Relation to External Objects* (Edinburgh, 1828, and numerous editions thereafter), for the seventeenth-century British philosopher John Locke, whose well-known *Essay Concerning Human Understanding* first appeared in 1690. A confusion of spine titles (*Combe on the Constitution, Locke on Understanding*) and the natural association between combs and locks could solely account for this lapse.

[*Mercury*, May 6, 1863]

Camp Meigs, Readville, May 4

Messrs. Editors:—The past week has been one of encouragement and interest to the 54th; our muster is now 868 men, and this week I hope to chronicle the pleasing intelligence, "the 54th is full." We have sufficient reason to warrant us in saying that such will be the case.

Fast Day was observed here by a respite from drilling in the forenoon, and a grand review in the afternoon. Indeed it looked like anything but a day of humiliation and prayer—it seemed more like a grand gala day, if judged by the number of visitors on the ground. The crowd was so great that the officers would allow no carriages within the lines. It would be safe to say that all Belknap street was here en masse.[20] It was indeed a pleasant scene to see the "boys" who had friends to see them, demolishing the good things brought them with such a keen relish; you may be sure they thought not of fasting. In the afternoon Gov. Andrew and Secretary Chase visited the camp, which was the occasion of the review mentioned above.[21] As the Governor entered the lines, attended by Brig. Gen. Pierce and staff, there arose a loud and enthusiastic cheer, long to be remembered. If there had been one present who asserts that black men are without military spirit, the spectacle in Camp Meigs last Thursday would have convinced him of his error.

Yesterday the men received their new arms. We are supplied with the Enfield rifle, made in 1853, so you may suppose they intend us to make good use of them; and I doubt not if the opportunity presents itself, they will be made good use of.

20. Belknap Street in Boston extended from Beacon to Cambridge streets in the West End. According to one writer, "From about 1830 till about 1892 more Negroes lived in the West End, beyond Joy St. and down along the northwesterly slope of Beacon Hill, to several blocks below Cambridge Street, than in any other section of Greater Boston" (John Daniels, *In Freedom's Birthplace: A Study of Boston Negroes* [Boston, 1914; New York, 1968], 143).

21. President Lincoln proclaimed April 30 as a day of national humiliation, fasting, and prayer. Samuel Portland Chase was a lawyer with strong anti-slavery sentiments then serving as secretary of the treasury in Lincoln's cabinet.

There was quite a number of visitors here yesterday, including Gov. Berry, of New Hampshire.[22] We have a new style of cooking department here, to be experimented upon. It is a large wagon, covered similar to an omnibus, with a stove and all the appurtenances of a well ordered kitchen. It is intended to move on the march. It will be a very handy affair, if adopted. So the 54th will be supplied with all the modern improvements.

Last Thursday I could not but put the question to myself, when I saw so many strong, able-bodied looking young men, why are you not here? why come as spectators when there is ample chance for you to become actors? I felt a mingled feeling of joy and sorrow—joy, because I felt the men who stood as actors in the scene were superior, in the eyes of all patriotic men, to those who came to see the show; sorrow, because these men had the effrontery to come here and look patronizingly upon those who are on the eve of going to secure them a home hereafter.

I must confess, it is enough to discourage real well wishers of the cause, to know that the "hub of the Universe" contributed only the small number of 80 men to a whole regiment.[23] It is a fact though, and the only way to make it otherwise, is to send at least 100 more men here, whose interests are identified with the State. The regiment will be full; but it would be more credit to the State if it were filled by her own colored citizens. When the war is over, and those who are spared to return shall march through the grand thoroughfares of our principal cities, ragged, lame, shoeless, and a banner tattered and torn by hostile balls, they then will learn who holds the highest place in the affections of a grateful people. What better reward is possible to conceive than the blessings of those we left behind in sorrow and tears; time, that great solver of events, will teach them this; if they suffer now, they would suffer more in the future, if we do not try now to avert it. It is rumored

22. Abolitionist Nathaniel Springer Berry was elected on the Republican ticket in 1861 and was considered one of the more effective "war governors."

23. Gooding is probably referring to Boston, which had the largest black population in the state but which, according to the roster of the regiment, contributed only about forty-five enlisted men from the city proper (James M. McPherson, *The Negro's Civil War: How American Negroes Felt and Acted During the War for the Union* [New York, 1965], appendix B; McKay, "Roster," in Emilio, *History of the Fifty-fourth*, 339–88).

we are to receive a flag today, but I cannot place any reliance in it. We have heard so many different rumors, about different subjects, that we are rather slow to believe anything we don't see. (Money especially.)

J. H. G.

[*Mercury*, May 11, 1863]

Camp Meigs, Readville, May 9

Messrs. Editors:—The past week has been one of progress with the 54th: 68 more men will make it a full regiment, if all the men are retained, which I think is rather doubtful, as there is about a dozen or more who, by the trying effects of camp life, are not physically able to be retained as good able soldiers. So far as physical ability is concerned and qualities of endurance as a regiment, the 54th will compare favorably with any ever raised in the State; indeed had every man been received who has applied, the regiment would have been filled at least three weeks since. Those having the raising of the regiment in charge are entitled to praise in not enlisting all sorts of men, regardless of their fitness to bear the hardships of military life, a striking contrast to the manner in which some of our regiments were raised. If they could only get 1000 men, they never thought of the fact that good sound men, although recruited slowly, would be better for themselves in the end. A number of regiments in the field, thinned out by sickness more than battle, had to be consolidated, so that the high "comish" in some cases will have to follow the unheroic paths of commerce or law once more. Surgeon General Dale paid an official visit to the camp last Monday and reviewed the battalion. He appears to seem satisfied that the boys will do.

That flag presentation didn't come off, and it is very probable it won't, or else it is such a big one it takes a long time to make it. Well, I suppose it is, and it will be bigger before we see it.

By the papers we see Richmond is not taken yet; it would be a little strange if the 54th were destined to tear down Jeff. Davis' nest.[24] I

24. Jefferson Davis, president of the Confederacy, had made Richmond, Virginia, his headquarters and capital since the end of May 1861.

think our boys would like such a job as that; they might not do it so scientifically as some, but they would never know when they were whipped, and that is the feeling which should pervade every man in the Union armies. Let every man feel that he has got a personal or family interest in this war, as the leaders of the South have, and with the immense armies, means and fleets the government have got, the rebellion would be speedily crushed. The American people, as a nation, knew not what they were fighting for till recently, and many have different opinions now as to the ends and results of the contest. But there is but two results possible, one is slavery and poverty and the other is liberty and prosperity. The latter can be preserved by oneness and singleness of purpose in regard to this contest, or the former will be sure, if love of place, prejudice and partisanship blind them so that they cannot see their way. Let every man of color consider that he has an interest in this war as well as the white man, and it will be well with them.

J. H. G.

[*Mercury*, May 18, 1863]

Camp Meigs, Readville, May 16

Messrs. Editors:—As we fondly expected last week, the 54th is now full, and as "Artemas" expresses it, "it slopt over," so the spilt ones are now the germ of another regiment, the 55th.

The Journal of Commerce, some weeks since, derided the idea of raising a colored regiment in the whole of the loyal States, but it was as near right that time as when it predicted McClellan would have to be recalled to save the nation from anarchy and ruin.[25] These old fogy sheets seem to think if they modify their opinions to the humane and progressive spirit of the times, they lay themselves open to the charge of inconsistency; they lose sight of the fact that to be thoroughly consis-

25. In the dark winter after the massive Union defeat at Fredericksburg, Virginia, on Dec. 13, 1862, it was rumored that the government at Washington was on the verge of collapse and that Gen. George Brinton McLellan, whom Lincoln had fired in November, might be recalled to head a military government (McPherson, *Battle Cry*, 574).

tent with their position as journalists, they should support what is right, regardless of party ties or Southern patronage. One who has any idea of the manner of mercantile transactions conducted in "Gotham,"[26] might suspect the mercantile mouth-piece was largely interested in the rise and fall of sugar, cotton, turpentine and other tropical commodities.

The battalion of cavalry left last Tuesday for Washington; that battalion was the first ever escorted by a black regiment, and I can assure you they seemed not ashamed of their escort. Gov. Andrew was down to see them off, and it was by his request that the 54th was detailed to give them a parting salute. Who says the world does not move?[27]

Col. Maggi was at camp last Tuesday afternoon; he happened to be present during the battalion drill; he said the men drilled splendidly. I think he must be a competent judge.[28]

The papers say we are to leave here the 20th, but where we are going they seem to know no more than we do. We have got a band, or at least the instruments; there are fifteen men taken from the regiment to form a band; Professor Bond is the instructor; by the frequency of practice he is maintaining, he appears to be determined to make them equal to any band he has formed or taught during the war. W[h]arton A. Williams, one of our New Bedford boys, is to be Band Sergeant.[29]

There is no more news of importance, so I will content myself till we march. The readers of the Mercury will be fully posted of our progress to our destination.

J. H. G.

26. New York City.

27. The 2d Massachusetts Cavalry, under Col. Charles R. Lowell, left Readville for the field on May 12. Emilio states "At noon the Fifty-fourth formed in great haste to escort the cavalry, and marched to their camp, only to learn that the Second had already departed" (*History of the Fifty-fourth*, 24).

28. Col. Albert C. Maggi, a resident of New Bedford, served in the Massachusetts 21st Volunteer Regiment and had just recently resigned as commander of the Massachusetts 33rd (Commonwealth of Massachusetts, Adjutant General's Office, *Massachusetts Soldiers, Sailors and Marines in the Civil War* [Norwood, Mass., 1931–35], 3: 538).

29. At a meeting held in Boston on May 21, subscribers to the fund for the 54th Regiment heard that the music committee had secured fifteen instruments and the services of Mr. Bond, an instructor (New Bedford *Mercury*, May 23, 1863).

[*Mercury*, May 20, 1863]

Camp Meigs, Readville, May 18

Messrs. Editors:—Today the long talked of presentation of flags came off. At 11 o'clock the column was formed, ready to receive His Excellency the Governor. Between four and five hundred people were on the ground before the hour fixed for the parade; when the 11 A.M. train stopped, there was a motley mass of people emerging from the cars, among which were the ladies of Boston, who were the makers of the colors, and the donors. Arrived upon the ground, it was a long time before sufficient space could be made to carry out the formalities; the colonel was obliged to order the commanders of two companies to march their commands to the front to make room for forming the square. After all the preliminaries were settled, Rev. Mr. Grimes, of Boston, offered a very impressive prayer.[30] The Governor and staff, Gen. Pierce and staff, with the whole regiment, during the prayer remained uncovered. The Governor then stepped forward and in substance spoke as follows:

Mr. Commander—Although the presentation of a stand of colors to a noble body of men is no new scene in this Commonwealth, this occasion is a novel and peculiar one—there is an importance attached to this occasion which never existed with any similar event. Today we recognize the right of every man in this Commonwealth to be a MAN and a citizen. We see before us a band of as noble men as ever came together for a great and glorious cause; they go not for themselves alone, but they go to vindicate a foul aspersion that they were not men; and I rejoice to see men from other states who have cast their lot in with ours—we welcome them as citizens of the Old Bay State. We not only see the germs of the elevation of a downtrodden and despised race, but a great and glorious future spread out before us, when the principles of right and justice shall govern our beloved country. You, Mr. Commander, have reason to be proud that you have the privilege of being the pioneer in this great and glorious cause, as the Chief of the Fifty

30. Rev. Leonard A. Grimes, born of free parents in Leesburg, Virginia, moved to Boston in 1848 and became active in the anti-slavery movement. He was pastor of the Twelfth Baptist Church there (Daniels, *In Freedom's Birthplace*, 452).

Fourth Regiment of Massachusetts Volunteers. And my earnest prayer is that you will ever have in view a lively interest in its efficiency and glory in the field, as you have thus far shown in its organization. I now have the honor, in behalf of the colored ladies of Boston, to present to you, sir, for the 54th regiment of Mass. volunteers, the American Flag; and before it shall ever be surrendered to the foes may its white stripes be spattered with the red blood of their brethren who bear it in the field. I now have the honor of presenting the 54th, through you, sir, in behalf of the Commonwealth, the arms of the State of Massachusetts; and I say today, from the beginning of this rebellion to the present day, that banner has never been surrendered to the foe; fifty-three regiments have marched from the old Bay State, but we have yet to learn that they ever surrendered that noble banner. Hold on to the staff, if every thread is blown away, your glory will be the same. Here is a banner, bearing for its emblem the Goddess of Liberty; take this, sir, in behalf of the colored ladies of Boston and the Commonwealth, for the 54th regiment Mass. volunteers. May you and your men prove that this emblem was never carried by worthier hands.

And here I have the solemn pleasure of presenting you, sir, in behalf of the near and dear relatives of one of Massachusetts noble soldier boys, who gave his life for his country's cause, Lieut. Putnam, the emblem which it bears, the symbol of the Christian, a Cross. While in the battle's rage, you cast your eyes on this Christian banner, remember, sir, the example of the gallant man who took it for his guide.[31] Though you fall in your country's defence, with a just and sincere appreciation of the teachings inculcated by that banner, your spirit will soar to that home in store for those who faithfully do their duty here to Humanity, their Country and their God!

And now let me thank you, sir, Mr. Commander, and your assistant officers, for the faithful discharge of the trust reposed in you all. I declare to you today, that the 54th regiment of volunteers will ever be to me a source of solicitude; it is an undertaking, which if it fails, I fail with it; not only myself in my official capacity, but thousands in the old Bay State will watch its progress with earnest, heartfelt interest; if on

31. Second Lt. William L. Putnam, a twenty-one-year-old law student from Boston, died Oct. 22, 1861, of wounds received the day before at Ball's Bluff, Virginia (*Massachusetts Soldiers, Sailors and Marines*, 2: 538).

the field, this noble Corps shall prove as valiant as it is proficient in discipline and drill, the fondest well wisher of this cause will be amply rewarded.

You Mr. Commander, have an important trust confided to you; your own honor as a man, and commander, the sound and wholesome discipline of a class unused to military life, that they as well as yourself, may add lustre to the glory of your native State.

Your country's honor, and the safety of these men, depend upon you; a nobler corps ne'er tread the soil of Massachusetts, and I am proud to say, much is due you for the military spirit they exhibit to-day; again [illegible] the flag.

Colonel Shaw responded in a [illegible] as follows:

It will be my earnest endeavors to faithfully perform all that is possible for the honor and glory of the 54th regiment volunteers; I consider it an honor to lead men, although many of them not citizens of Massachusetts, who exhibit such unmistakable evidences of patriotism; and I will take this occasion to express my sincere thanks to the officers, and men, for their untiring efforts to assist me in maintaining order, and a faithful discharge of every duty.

Mr. I.D. Hall and Mr. John Goings will please accept the thanks of Company C, for a present of tobacco, two twenty-five pound boxes; we can assure them it is very acceptable, as many of us have not had any tobacco for some time.[32]

J. H. G.

[*Mercury*, May 26, 1863]

Camp Meigs, Readville, May 24, 1863

Messrs. Editors:—My last letter I had supposed would be the last to be written from this camp, but so much for "newspaper yarns," we are still here. This week has been in the estimation of the men, the greatest in the history of regiments, the presentation of colors, an excursion, and last, but not least, the payment of the State bounty. We had almost despaired of ever getting the last mentioned excitement, but it has

32. Isaac D. Hall owned a wholesale grocery bearing his name at 60 Union Street, New Bedford. John Goings was a servant in the household of a prominent New Bedford family (*New Bedford Directory* [New Bedford, 1859]).

come, and many a wife and widowed mother will have for a little while, at least something to purchase bread; on the whole, I think, there has more money been sent home to relatives of men in this regiment than any other which has been paid their bounty. But of course among a thousand men, there must be a large amount of money wasted; the sutler, patent jewelry venders, watch pedlars and many other kinds of pedlars are reaping a rich harvest. Why, it is enough to make a "feller" love "human natur" to see how very obliging the said pedlars are; they will even condescend to sell a pair of boots worth $4 for the moderate sum of $8, and other traders ask a proportionate sum. Gen. Pierce put a veto on them though, after he found out how the cat was jumping; he told one man he should sell nothing to the men unless he received an order from himself and agree[d] to conform to a reasonable price, the General to determine the price. The men will appreciate his kindness after their greenbacks are gone.

We have received marching orders; the order was read at dress parade last Thursday, so next Sunday I think we shall be on our way to Dixie. We have crowds of visitors daily, drawn, no doubt, by the great reputation the regiment is gaining for proficiency in drill. The band is a success. It is only ten days since they first commenced practice, but they have played on dress parade three times. It seems that most every man in the regiment vies with each other in excellence in whatever they undertake. It is, I think, one of the best guarantees that the 54th will be a credit to old Massachusetts wherever it goes. The citizens of this Commonwealth need not be ashamed of the 54th now; and if the regiment will be allowed a chance, I feel confident the Colored Volunteers will add glory to her already bright name. There is not a man in the regiment who does not appreciate the difficulties, the dangers, and maybe ignoble death that awaits him, if captured by the foe, and they will die upon the field rather than be hanged like a dog; and when a thousand men are fighting for a very existence, who dare say them men won't fight determinedly? The greatest difficulty will be to stop them.[33]

J. H. G.

33. The Confederates refused to recognize captured black soldiers as legitimate prisoners of war and threatened to enslave or execute them.

2

A First Class Regiment
South Carolina and Georgia, June 1863

General David Hunter, command-ing the Department of the South, requested in mid-May that the Fifty-fourth Regiment be sent to South Carolina, and the regiment prepared to depart. Early on the morning of May 28 the men boarded a train for Boston, then marched to the State House along a route lined with cheering specta-tors and decorated with flags. There they joined Governor An-drew and his party and proceeded to the Common for a review of the regiment.

Their reception was enthusias-tic: "vast crowds lined the streets where the regiment was to pass, and the Common was crowded with an immense number of peo-ple, such as only the 4th of July or some rare event causes to assem-ble."[1] Later they marched down to Battery Wharf and boarded the steamer DeMolay, bound for the south.

[*Mercury*, June 19, 1863]

Port Royal, June 3

Messrs. Editors:—After a long passage of seven days, we have arrived at Port Royal.[2] We are still on board the vessel, and I write my

1. Boston *Evening Journal*, May 28, 1863, as quoted in Cornish, *Sable Arm*, 148.
2. The steamer *De Molay*, described by Emilio as a "commodious, new, and excellent transport," had brought the regiment to the Union headquarters of the Department of the South. Hilton Head lies at the entrance to Port Royal harbor; Beaufort is farther

first letter on the top of my knapsack, with one of the loudest noises around me ever heard, and heat enough to make a fellow contemplate the place prepared for the ungodly. There is nothing interesting to write as yet, for the very good reason that we have none of us been ashore. I write this letter to let the friends of the men know that we are all safe, except one, who jumped overboard the first night out from Boston. I think he must have been cracked or drunk, more likely the latter.[3] The men are all in good health and spirits, not one man in the whole regiment being now on the sick list. After we are quartered on shore, and have an opportunity to look around, you may expect better letters.

J. H. G.

Beaufort, S. C., June 8th

Messrs. Editors:—We arrived at this town on the evening of the 4th, not debarking at Hilton Head. On the morning of the 5th, we left the steamer and marched to our camp ground about a quarter of a mile out of the town, near the 55th Pennsylvania and 8th Maine regiments. Our reception was almost as enthusiastic here in Beaufort, as our departure from Boston was. You know probably how universal the enthusiasm was in Boston. The 54th has already won the reputation here of being a first class regiment, both in drill, discipline and physical condition. When the 54th marched through the streets of this town, the citizens and soldiers lined the walks, to get a look at the first black regiment from the North.[4] The contrabands did not believe we were coming; one of them said, "I nebber bleeve black Yankee comee here help culer

---

inland on the north side of Port Royal Island. Seventy miles south of Charleston, the area was captured by the Union navy in November 1861 and became the base of operations for both the army and the blockade fleet (Emilio, *History of the Fifty-fourth*, 33; William C. Davis, *Stand in the Day of Battle*, vol. 2 of *The Imperiled Union, 1861–1865* [Garden City, N.Y., 1983], 50).

3. According to Emilio the voyage was without incident (*History of the Fifty-fourth*, 36).

4. Emilio writes that the regiment landed at 5 A.M., too early in the day to attract the attention of any but a few loiterers. It had arrived the night before, as Col. James Montgomery and the 2d South Carolina (Colored) Regiment were debarking with several hundred contrabands.

men." They think now the kingdom is coming sure enough. The yarns the copperhead press have so studiously spun, that the slaves were better satisfied in their old condition than under the present order of things, is all bosh. So far as I have seen, they appear to understand the causes of the war better than a great many Northern editors. South Carolina was the pioneer in the war, and she had a double reason for it. According to one of the slaves showing, there had been a conspiracy hatching among the slaves, as far back as 1856, the year Fremont was up for the Presidency.[5] The negroes had heard through their masters that Fremont was a "damned abolitionist," they then began to lay plans to escape, or if necessary to fight. In December, 1856, after the defeat of the Republicans, one Prince Rivers went to Charleston, in the name of an organized committee, praying the Governor of the State to recommend the legislature to so modify some certain statutes that the negroes could live a little more like civilized people. The Governor sent him home to his master, telling him the State could not interfere with the relations existing between master and slave. Soon after that, every gun, pistol or other weapon was taken from the slaves; but the chivalry took fine care to say nothing about it in the papers. The people of the North knew nothing of these things.[6]

The slaves, hereabouts, are working for the government mostly, although they can make a pretty snug little sum, peddling among the soldiers, selling fruit, &c.

The 2d South Carolina volunteers have made a successful expedition. Col. Montgomery left with his regiment May 1st, in three small steamers, accompanied by Capt. Brayton of the Rhode Island artillery with one section of his command; the next morning he anchored in the Combahee river, thirty miles from Beaufort and twenty from Charleston, and thirteen from Asheepoo, on the Charleston and Savannah railroad. The village on the river is approached by three different roads; one from Field's Point, where the rebels had built a battery, but had

5. John Charles Fremont, explorer of the American West and one of California's first senators (1850–1851), was nominated by the new Republican party in 1856 and ran unsuccessfully against James Buchanan. During the Civil War he was put in charge of the Western Department until his radical policy of freeing the slaves and confiscating slaveowners' property led to his removal in late summer 1861.

6. A Prince Rivers was later a color sergeant in Col. Thomas W. Higginson's 1st South Carolina Regiment (Cornish, *Sable Arm*, 91, 134).

deserted it; one from Tar Bluff, two miles above Field's Point and one from Combahee Ferry, six miles further up the river.

According to plans laid beforehand, Col. Montgomery took possession of the three approaches at one time. Capt. Thompson, with one company was placed in the earthworks at Field's Point; Capt. Carver, with Co. E. was placed in the rifle pits at Tar Bluff; and, with the balance of the force, Col. M. proceeded to Combahee Ferry, and with the guns of the John Adams,[7] and two howitzers, under command of Capt. Brayton, completely covered the road and the approaches to the bridge. At Asheepoo the rebels had three regiments of infantry, one battalion of cavalry, and a field battery of artillery. As Capt. Thompson advanced up the road from Field's Point, cavalry came in sight, but a few well-directed volleys sent them back in confusion to their stronghold at Asheepoo. At half past three a battery of six pieces opened fire upon them, but not a man flinched, but poured their fire in upon the rebels, killing and wounding a number. At this stage of affairs, the Harriet A. Weed[8] came up the river and poured a few shells in the midst of the rebels, causing them to retreat hastily. The raid commenced in earnest then, the soldiers scattered in every direction, burning and destroying everything of value they came across. Thirty-four large mansions, belonging to notorious rebels, were burned to the ground. After scattering the rebel artillery, the Harriet A. Weed tied up opposite a large plantation, owned by Nicholas Kirkland. Major Corwin, in command of companies R and C, soon effected a landing, without opposition. The white inhabitants, terrified at seeing armed negroes in their midst, fled in all directions, while the blacks ran for the boats, welcoming the soldiers as their deliverers. After destroying all they could not bring away, the expedition returned to Beaufort Wednesday evening, with over $15,000 worth of property and 840 slaves.[9] Over 400

7. An armed transport vessel (Emilio, *History of the Fifty-fourth*, 40).

8. The *Harriet A. Weed* was a U.S. Army steamer. She was later destroyed by a torpedo in St. John's River, Florida, on May 10, 1864 (*Official Records of the Union and Confederate Navies in the War of the Rebellion*, 30 vols. [Washington, 1894–1922], series 1, vol. 15, pp. 426–27); hereafter cited as *ORN*, with series number followed by volume and pages.

9. Col. James Montgomery's report on this expedition was not found when the *Official Records* were being compiled. For the Confederate side of the story, however, see *War of*

of the captured slaves have been enlisted in the 3d S. C. regiment; the rest of the number being women and children and old men. Col. M. left yesterday on another expedition, and the 54th is ordered for active service. We leave tonight for, the Lord knows where, but we shall try to uphold the honor of the Old Bay State wherever we go.

The wagons are being packed, so I must close.

J. H. G.

[*Mercury*, June 30, 1863]

St. Simon's Island, Ga., June 14, 1863

Messrs. Editors:—As intimated in my last letter, we left Beaufort last Monday morning. We did not know where we were going, and never found out until we dropped anchor off this Island on the morning of the 9th.[10] After being transferred to a steamer of lighter draught, we were landed about nine miles up the river from the anchorage. Here I may say, I could hardly determine whether we were bound up or down the river, it is so crooked. The next day, after we arrived here, the 2nd South Carolina regiment, the 2nd R.I. battery, and 8 companies of the 54th started on an expedition.[11] We landed on the main land, at a small town, named Darien, about 50 miles from here by water, but only about 20 miles over land. The force took the water route, as it is impracticable to get to it over land, the country being so marshy, crossed by numberless little creeks running through it. The rebels must have left the place when they saw such a large force concentrating on St. Simon's Island the day before, supposing they would be attacked. After our forces landed, there was not more than 20 inhabitants to be seen in the place,

---

the Rebellion . . . *Official Records of the Union and Confederate Armies*, 128 vols. (Washington, 1880–1901), series 1, vol. 14, pp. 291–308; hereafter cited as *ORA*, with series number followed by volume, part number if there is one, and pages.

10. St. Simon's Island, Georgia, is south of Savannah at the mouth of the Altamaha River. In 1863, the island had a number of deserted plantations, including that of Pierce Butler, whose wife, Fanny Kemble, wrote of her experiences there in *Journal of a Residence on a Georgian Plantation, in 1838–39* (1863) (Emilio, *History of the Fifty-fourth*, 45).

11. According to Emilio, Companies F and C were left behind as camp guard. He gives a full description of the raid on Darien (ibid., 40–44).

the most of those were slaves and women; so there was no chance to show what sort of fighting material the Fifty-Fourth is made of. The fruits of the expedition are the capture of one schooner and a flat boat, loaded with cotton, about 20 barrels of turpentine, eight hogsheads of rosin, about a dozen cows, 50 or 60 sheep and 20 head of beeves; books, pictures, furniture and household property were burned. The town of Darien is now no more; the flames could be distinctly seen from the camp on the Island from three o'clock in the afternoon till daylight the next morning.

We are to go on another expedition next week, into the interior. It is rumored we are to try to take possession of a railroad between Savannah and some point south, probably Mobile. We all hope the rebels will make a stand, so that we may have a good chance to empty our cartridge boxes.

Talking about Southern scenery! Well, all I have seen of it yet is not calculated to make me eulogize its beauties. If a person were to ask me what I saw South, I should tell him stink weed, sand, rattlesnakes, and alligators. To tell the honest truth, our boys out on picket look sharper for snakes than they do for rebels.[12]

In a church yard here, I saw a stone bearing this inscription, "James Gould, born at Granville, Mass., 1806, died 1862"; another was, "Lieut. Col. Wardrobe, of his B[ritish] M[ajesty's] service, died 1812"; another, "James Wyley, born at Fitchburg, Mass., 1822, died February, 1863."

J. H. G.

[*Mercury,* July 8, 1863]

St. Simon's Island, Ga., June 22

Messrs. Editors:—Since my last letter, there has been nothing important occurred in this department that I am aware of. In fact if anything important were to happen, in which our regiment was not concerned, you in the North would be more likely to be posted in regard to it, than we should, isolated as we are.

---

12. On the other hand Captain Emilio felt that "St. Simon's came nearer a realization of the ideal Eden than one could hope to find the second time" (ibid., 45).

Of course the opposition press have heard of the burning of Darien, by the "Nigger guerillas," and commented on it, as an "act of Vandalism" and all that sort of thing; manufactured capital enough to bring "Nigger worshippers" in contempt, in the opinion of gouty "conservatives," and wrought Wood and Co.'s followers up to that delightful point, of commanding the Powers that be to stop enlisting the "impediments to civilization" instanter.[13] How they must have harrowed the feelings of sentimental young ladies by informing them how those "ruthless heathens," unmoved by the entreaties of terror stricken damsels, slew their gallant lovers in cold blood; and then exhausted the vocabulary of unmentionable adjectives on the horrified maidens after their protectors were slain. Of course they made it appear to credulous people that Darien was a place rivaling New York, in commercial importance, and the peer of Rome or Athens, in historical value. But they did not intimate that one of the ships, destroyed by the rebel pirates, might possibly be worth nearly as much as the village of Darien. Oh no! what the people of the North has lost is nothing, because what the North lost was stolen by our misguided brethern.[14]

But turn the tables—say the troops here should be captured by the rebels, (of course they would hang them every one), the copperhead press would treat that as an unimportant item, or some of them would say probably, "we are glad of it—that is a cheaper way of getting rid of them, than expending money to send them to President Lincoln's Paradise in Central America, or to colonize them at Timbuctoo or Sahara."[15]

13. Fernando Wood, sometime congressman, Tammany Hall leader, and mayor of New York, had joined with Clement Vallandigham to organize the Peace Democrats in 1863. His brother Benjamin owned a Copperhead New York paper, the *Daily News*.

14. Nevertheless even Colonel Shaw felt that Montgomery had gone too far in destroying Darien, and he tried to dissociate himself from what he believed to be sheer vandalism, carried out for personal satisfaction rather than military necessity (Emilio, *History of the Fifty-fourth*, 44).

15. The nineteenth century saw a number of efforts to colonize free blacks from the United States in places like Sierra Leone, Liberia, and Haiti. In mid-August 1862, President Lincoln met with five blacks from the District of Columbia and expressed his feeling that complete separation of the races was the only solution to the problem of inequality stemming from physical differences. His proposal that blacks move to Central America, where newly opened coal mines would provide opportunities for employment, was not well received. One who spoke out against the plan wrote, "Good sir, if you have

But we all know they must say something, or people will think they are losing ground; they must keep up the appearance of knowing considerable, if not more, as one instance will show. A man living in Pennsylvania wrote to one of the men in this regiment that things had turned out just as he had predicted months ago; that the United States had repudiated the black troops and would never pay them the first red cent; that Gov. Andrew had disbanded his second party of "Pet Lambs" and advised the men to skedaddle, as the government would not have any power to punish them; in fact such an organization as the 54th regiment Mass. vols. was not known officially by the War Department. Now don't you think that man was hired to write such stuff as that? The object is obvious; it is to create a spirit of insubordination among the men, so that the copperheads may have a better excuse to call for the disbanding of colored regiments in the field. Oh, there are some grand rascals out of State Prison! The scamp who wrote that letter signed no full name to it; it was dated from Susquehanna Co., Pa., no town, but the postmark was Philadelphia. Whoever he is, it is evident he has played at more than one game in his life, for the receiver of the letter does not know whose handwriting it is. We are expecting to make a movement now hourly; the regiment are only waiting for the return of the commanding officer, with his instructions. There sounds the long roll! I must close.

J. H. G.

St. Helena Island, S.C., June 29

Messrs. Editors:—Instead of going on another expedition, as we all expected and hoped, we find ourselves at the headquarters of the department, and great changes made in commanders; in fact, the changes had been made at least two weeks before we knew anything of them.[16] It is probable that the change of commander has made some change in

---

any nearer friends than we are, let them have that coal-digging job" (*National Anti-Slavery Standard*, Sept. 6, 1862, as quoted in McPherson, *The Negro's Civil War*, 93).

16. On June 12, 1863, Brig. Gen. Quincy Adams Gillmore superseded Maj. Gen. David Hunter in command of the Department of the South. News of this appointment, as well as that of Adm. John A. Dahlgren to relieve Admiral DuPont as commander of the South Atlantic blockading squadron, was received on June 23 (*ORA* 1, 28.1: 1; Emilio, *History of the Fifty-fourth*, 46).

the operations in this department, for this summer at least. But from appearances there must be something definite in contemplation, from the fact that all the surplus troops are being concentrated on this island ready for a movement at the shortest notice; either to act on the offensive, at some weak point—as the force here is not large enough to make any grand movement—or to be transported wherever the urgency of the case may require out of this department; but it is safe to say the latter conjecture is the most probable one.

Yesterday there was a terrific thunder storm here. A man in the 76th Pa. regiment was killed by lightening, and 15 more were stunned at the same time, besides exploding 80 boxes of cartridges.

A sergeant in the 1st regiment S. C. Volunteers has been sentenced to be hung for mutiny, or inciting some of the men to mutinous conduct.

The rebel ram Atlanta, taken off the Savannah river, has been pronounced unseaworthy by the Naval Guard. It was the intention of the rebels to play hob with the Yankees. The plan was first, to pay a compliment to Col. Montgomery, then on St. Simon's Island, and hang his whole force, then come up and clear out Port Royal harbour, raise the blockade at Charleston, and I don't know but they would have gone on capturing till they reached Boston, according to their story. Probably that was one of the plans to assist in raising their volunteer navy. They have another ram underway at Savannah, but she will not be completed for some time.[17]

J. H. G.

17. The ram *Atlanta* was a Confederate man-of-war converted from the British iron steamer *Fingal* that had run the blockade of Savannah in November 1861. The conversion project, which took more than a year, was paid for with funds raised by the people of Savannah. Although vastly superior in strength, *Atlanta* was captured by the Union monitor *Weehawken* in Wassaw Sound, June 17, 1863, on her first attempt to elude the blockade. (For an eyewitness account of the battle see Alvah F. Hunter, *A Year on a Monitor and the Destruction of Fort Sumter* [Columbia, S.C., 1987], 73–86. Also, report of Capt. John Rodgers, U.S. Navy, commanding U.S.S. *Weehawken* in *ORN* 1, 14:265–66.)

3

Something Stirring to Record
Charleston, South Carolina, July 1863

The capture of Charleston was high on the list of federal priorities. There the first shots of the war had been fired in April 1861; there the first humiliating Union defeat occurred when Fort Sumter fell. For the North, Charleston symbolized the intransigence and arrogance of the South.

Charleston was also an important target as a shipping and communications center. Its harbor, with three approach channels and constantly shifting shoals and current, was virtually impossible to seal off from the sea. Blockade runners kept Charleston supplied with cargoes from abroad, and rail connections with Savannah and Atlanta provided the means to distribute these supplies more widely.

The city occupies a narrow peninsula formed by the Ashley and Cooper rivers which flow into the basin that makes up Charleston Harbor. The entrance to the harbor, about seven miles from the city, is formed by Sullivan's Island on the north and Morris Island on the south. A sand bar stretches across its mouth.

Inside the bar three main fortresses guarded the harbor entrance: Fort Moultrie on Sullivan's Island; Fort Johnson located on James Island to the east of Morris Island; and Fort Sumter, built on a shoal midway between the two and on the south side of the ship channel.

The land approaches to Charleston from the south were a group of low-lying islands crisscrossed by innumerable creeks and inlets and dotted with virtually impassable marshes that sometimes stretched for miles. It was here that the War Department had determined to conduct a major campaign in the spring of 1863.

Initially the army was to play a secondary role, with a force standing by to occupy Charleston once the city's guns had been silenced by naval bombardment. After an unsuccessful engagement on April 7, when the attacking United States fleet managed to get off only 139 shots, and was severely damaged in the process, a different plan was adopted with the army in the lead.

The first target was to be Morris Island and its primary defense, Fort Wagner. Once that position was secured Union guns would demolish Fort Sumter, allowing the fleet to enter the inner harbor. With continued artillery support from Morris Island the ironclads and monitors were then to remove the channel obstructions, run by the Confederate batteries on James and Sullivan's islands, and take Charleston.

The opposing armies were each commanded by military engineers experienced in the construction of batteries and in bombardment. Brigadier General Quincy Adams Gillmore had reduced Fort Pulaski, down river from Savannah, in two days the previous year. Confederate General Pierre Gustave Toutant Beauregard had been responsible for the bombardment and subsequent fall of Fort Sum-

ter, marking the beginning of the war, in April 1861. Since his recall to Charleston in the fall of 1862, he had worked steadily to increase the size and strength of the city's batteries. Beauregard had also filled the harbor with mines and other submerged obstructions.

Fort Wagner was extended to reach across the narrow island from the ocean on the east to a marsh on the west, and was equipped with eleven heavy guns plus mobile field pieces. A huge bombproof that could shelter an entire regiment was constructed. The only approach to this formidable work was from the south over a stretch of beach narrowed by spring storms to about one hundred feet across.

The staging area for the Union attack was Folly Island, below Lighthouse Inlet. South from there, all the way to Florida, the coast was under Union control. During late June and early July ordnance and troops were gathered to await the coming operations.

The first assault against Morris Island and Fort Wagner took place on July 10 and succeeded in driving the Confederates up the beach, reaching within several hundred yards of the fort before being stopped by heavy fire. Gillmore

then chose to let his men rest and
wait for the next day to renew the
attack—but it was an attack that
failed. Union casualties totaled
339 men to the Confederates' 12.[1]

Meanwhile, the men of the Fifty-
fourth were transported to James
Island, where they fought in an en-

gagement; they then made their
way to Morris Island. Arriving
on July 18, the regiment had been
three days with little rest and
twenty-four hours without food.
That evening the second assault on
Wagner began.

[*Mercury*, August 1, 1863]

Morris Island, July 20, 1863

Messrs. Editors:—At last we have something stirring to record. The
54th, the past week, has proved itself twice in battle. The first was on
James Island on the morning of the 16th. There were four companies of
the 54th on picket duty at the time; our picket lines extending to the
right of the rebel battery, which commands the approach to Charleston
through the Edisto river.[2] About 3 o'clock in the morning, the rebels
began harassing our pickets on the right, intending, no doubt, to drive
them in, so that by daylight the coast would be clear to rush their main
force down on us, and take us by surprise. They did not suppose we had
any considerable force to the rear of our pickets on the right, as Gen.
Stevenson's brigade was plain in sight on the left; and their plan, I
suppose, was to rush down and cut Gen. Stevenson off.[3] They made a
mistake—instead of returning fire, the officer in charge of the pickets
directed the men to lie down under cover of a hedge, rightly expecting

1. Peter M. Chaitin and the Editors of Time-Life Books, *The Coastal War: Chesapeake
Bay to Rio Grande* (Alexandria, Va., 1984), 124.
2. Four companies, D, F, I, and K, picketed on July 11. On July 16 the companies
detailed for picket were B, H, and K according to Emilio. The rebel battery, Fort
Pemberton, was on the Stono River, which forms the western boundary of James Island.
The Edisto River is farther south. An attack on Charleston from James Island was
considered by Confederate general Beauregard to be the most serious threat to the safety
of the city (*History of the Fifty-fourth*, 53–55).
3. Brig. Gen. Thomas G. Stevenson led a brigade consisting of the 24th Massachusetts,
10th Connecticut, and 97th Pennsylvania regiments (ibid., 53).

the rebels to advance by degrees toward our lines. As he expected, at daylight they were within 600 yards of the picket line, when our men rose and poured a volley into them. That was something the rebels didn't expect—their line of skirmishers was completely broken; our men then began to fall back gradually on our line of battle, as the rebels were advancing their main force on to them. On they came, with six pieces of artillery and four thousand infantry, leaving a heavy force to drive Gen. Stevenson on the left. As their force advanced on our right, the boys held them in check like veterans; but of course they were falling back all the time, and fighting too. After the officers saw there was no chance for their men, they ordered them to move on to a creek under cover of the gunboats. When the rebels got within 900 yards of our line of battle, the right wing of Gen. Terry's brigade gave them three volleys, which checked their advance.[4] They then made a stand with their artillery and began shelling us, but it had no effect on our forces, as the rebels fired too high. The 6th Connecticut battery then opened fire on them from the right, the John Adams and May Flower from the creek between James and Cole Islands, and the Pawnee and a mortar schooner from the Edisto [i.e., Stono], when the rebels began a hasty retreat.[5] It was a warmer reception than they had expected. Our loss in the skirmishing before the battle, so far as we can ascertain, was nine killed, 13 wounded, and 17 missing, either killed or taken prisoners; but more probably they were driven into the creek and drowned. Sergeant Wilson, of Co. H, was called upon to surrender, but would not; he shot four men before he was taken. After he was taken they ordered him to give up his pistol which he refused to do, when he was shot through the head.[6]

4. Brig. Gen. Alfred H. Terry was commanding a division of 4,000 men consisting of three brigades: Brig. Gen. Stevenson's; Col. W. W. H. Davis's, comprising the 52nd and 104th Pennsylvania and the 56th New York; and Col. James Montgomery's, composed of the 54th Massachusetts and the 2d South Carolina (ibid., 53).

5. *John Adams* and *May Flower* were armed transports; *Pawnee*, a gunboat (ibid., 56).

6. The adjutant general of Massachusetts gave the 54th's loss as fourteen killed, eighteen wounded, and thirteen missing. Sgt. Joseph D. Wilson, twenty-five years old, was expert in the use of the musket, having previously been employed with the Ellsworth Zouaves of Chicago. Emilio says he disabled three men while bravely resisting capture (ibid., 63, 58).

The men of the 54th behaved gallantly on the occasion—so the Generals say. It is not for us to blow our horn; but when a regiment of white men gave us three cheers as we were passing them, it shows that we did our duty as men should.

I shall pass over the incidents of that day, as regards individuals, to speak of a greater and more terrible ordeal the 54th regiment has passed through. I shall say nothing now of how we came from James to Morris Island; suffice it to say, on Saturday afternoon we were marched up past our batteries, amid the cheers of the officers and soldiers. We wondered what they were all cheering for, but we soon found out. Gen. Strong rode up, and we halted. Well, you had better believe there was some guessing what we were to do. Gen. Strong asked us if we would follow him into Fort Wagner. Every man said, yes—we were ready to follow wherever we were led.[7] You may all know Fort Wagner is the Sebastopol of the rebels; but we went at it, over the ditch and on to the parapet through a deadly fire; but we could not get into the fort. We met the foe on the parapet of Wagner with the bayonet—we were exposed to a murderous fire from the batteries of the fort, from our Monitors and our land batteries, as they did not cease firing soon enough. Mortal men could not stand such a fire, and the assault on Wagner was a failure. The 9th Me., 10th Conn., 63d Ohio, 48th and 100th N.Y. were to support us in the assault; but after we made the first charge, everything was in such confusion that we could hardly tell where the reserve was.[8] At the first charge the 54th rushed to within twenty yards of the ditches, and, as might be expected of raw recruits, wavered—but at the second advance they gained the parapet. The color bearer of the State colors was killed on the parapet. Col. Shaw seized the staff when the standard

7. Brig. Gen. George C. Strong led the assault on Fort Wagner with a brigade consisting of the 54th Massachusetts, the 6th and a battalion of the 7th Connecticut, the 48th New York, the 3rd New Hampshire, the 9th Maine, and the 76th Pennsylvania regiments (*ORA* 1, 28.1: 15).

8. The official report states that General Strong's force was supported by Colonel Putnam's brigade consisting of his own regiment (the 7th New Hampshire) and the 100th New York and the 62nd and 67th Ohio. These were all small regiments (*ORA* 1, 28.1: 5). According to Emilio a third, or reserve, brigade under Brig. Gen. Thomas G. Stevenson included the 24th Massachusetts, 10th Connecticut, 97th Pennsylvania, and 2d South Carolina regiments (*History of the Fifty-fourth*, 74).

bearer fell, and in less than a minute after, the Colonel fell himself. When the men saw their gallant leader fall, they made a desperate effort to get him out, but they were either shot down, or reeled in the ditch below. One man succeeded in getting hold of the State color staff, but the color was completely torn to pieces.[9]

I have no more paper here at present, as all our baggage is at St. Helena yet; so I cannot further particularize in this letter. Lieut. Grace was knocked down by a piece of shell, but he is not injured. He showed himself a great deal braver and cooler than any line officer.

J. H. G.

Our correspondent gives a list of killed, wounded and missing. It is the same that we have already published. [*Mercury* Editor]

"They mowed us down like grass" one survivor wrote to his mother; and Lieutenant Grace gave the following account to Brigadier General Pierce:

Knowing your deep interest in the officers and men of the Regiment, I thought I would let you know how we are after our Skirmish and retreat from James Island and Fight at Morris Island. We were on the move three days and nights before the Fight on this Island. When we arrived here, we were very much exhausted, tired and hungry, not having any thing to eat for twenty four hours. I simply speak of this to let you know what condition we were in before the Fight. We arrived on the Island about 3 o'clock, rested a short time, and then moved forward to the upper end of the Island (the Island is about four miles long). When we arrived within one thousand yards of Fort Wagner, we laid down waiting for our support to come up. We laid there about thirty minutes when we were ordered to rise up and charge on the works, which we did at double quick time with a

9. Sgt. William H. Carney of New Bedford carried the national colors to the parapet. Later, although severely wounded, he managed to bring them back to the rear, with the words "Boys, the old flag never touched the ground." For his courage and gallantry Carney was awarded both the Gillmore Medal and the Medal of Honor. He was one of four enlisted men from the 54th who received the former, and the first person of African descent to be awarded the latter (Ellis, *History of New Bedford and Vicinity*, 349).

tremendous scream. When we arrived within a short distance of the works, the Rebels opened on us with grape and canister accompanied with a thousand muskets, mowing our men down by the hundreds. This caused us to fall back a little, but we soon made another rush to the works, when we received another tremendous discharge of musketry, and also grape and canister. Such a tremendous fire right in our faces caused us to fall back, which we did in very good order. Our men are highly spoken of by military men as showing great bravery. They did fight when they were in front of the works [and a] good many of our men went on to the works and fought hand to hand with the Enemy.[10]

[*Mercury*, August 4, 1863]

Morris Island, July 24

Messrs. Editors:—Since my letter of the 20th last, our forces have been busily engaged, preparing for the grand sortie on Wagner and Sumter. When everything is complete, you may expect to hear of decisive results. It is very probable that Fort Wagner would have been in our possession now, had the rebels not sent a flag-of-truce boat out on the 22d inst. to exchange prisoners. The monitors, gunboats and batteries were blazing away on her (Wagner) that forenoon, and from the look of things, it seemed as though they were in a pretty tight place. I do not think, with the vast preparations now being made, that Wagner can hold out 48 hours if our side push matters a little when they do begin. Ere this meets the eyes of the readers of the Mercury, the Union troops may garrison both forts, Wagner and Sumter; but the people at home must not expect Charleston to be taken in two minutes, for even if Forts Wagner and Sumter are soon reduced, there is still a few miles between Sumter and the city, backed by heavy batteries on each shore. Winning victories by theory, in easy chairs at home, and fighting to win them on the field, are different things.

10. These extracts of letters from an unidentified soldier and from Lt. James W. Grace, Company C, 54th Regiment to Brig. Gen. R. A. Pierce, Readville, July 22, 1863, can be found in the Camp Meigs records, in Richard A. Pierce Papers, New Bedford Free Public Library.

We have since learned by the flag-of-truce boat that Colonel Shaw is dead—he was buried in a trench with 45 of his men! not even the commonest respect paid to his rank. Such conduct is in striking contrast to the respect paid a rebel Major, who was killed on James Island. The Commander of the 54th regiment had the deceased rebel officer buried with all the honors of war granted by the regulations; and they have returned the compliment by tossing him into a ditch.

We hope the London Times will make note of that fact. They did not say how many of our men they had buried, beyond the 45 with the Colonel, nor how many of them they have as prisoners; they merely said they would not exchange them then, but should hold them for future consideration. So we can give no definite news of those who are killed or prisoners. We have never been allowed to approach near enough to hold any parley with them since the night of the assault. It seems though, from the proceedings since the truce, that there might have been some "kid glove handling" of the negro volunteer question, as the two boats were side by side nearly three hours; though I may be wrong in my surmises. But since that day our regiment has not been out on picket duty, either as outposts or reserves; and this may be prompted by a desire of those in charge not to place a regiment of black men in an exposed position under such peculiar circumstances, until they know definitely what is to be the fate of those in the hands of the rebels.[11] If such be the case I think it is for the best. The regiment is hardly fit for service in the field at present for want of officers. Capts. Russell and

11. The Confederate threat to enslave or execute black soldiers in the Union army and to punish their officers as felons had reportedly been carried out from time to time in the South. War Department General Orders, No. 100, "Instructions for the Government of the Armies of the United States in the Field" issued April 24, 1863, had attempted to deter the rebels by promising the severest retaliation, i.e., death, for such crimes against the laws of nations. What was needed now, many Northerners felt, was a prompt, vigorous reminder. Thus on July 30 President Lincoln issued a proclamation ordering that "for every soldier of the United States killed in violation of the laws of war, a Rebel soldier shall be executed, and for every one enslaved by the enemy or sold into slavery, a Rebel soldier shall be placed at hard labor on the public works, and continue at such labor until the other shall be released and receive the treatment due a prisoner of war" (quoted in Emilio, *History of the Fifty-fourth*, 96–97). The full text of General Orders No. 100 is in *ORA* 3, 3: 148–64. For a further discussion of the Negro prisoner of war problem see Cornish, *Sable Arm*, 157–80.

Simpkins have never been heard of since the memorable night of the 18th. All the other company commanders are so severely wounded that it is feared some of them will never be able to resume the field again, and it is to be hoped that the steps for reorganizing the regiment will be speedily taken. It is due to what few officers we have left with us, to reward them with a step higher up the ladder. Col. Littlefield, of the 3d S.C. Regiment, has temporary charge of the 54th.[12]

I did intend to give you an account of our evacuation of James Island; but as we may have occasion to "play it over again," for strategic reasons, I'll keep dark on it.[13]

In my last letter I put down Abram P. Torrance as killed. I have subsequently learned that he is wounded, and is in the hospital at Beaufort. The rest of the list is, I think, correct. The total number of men now killed, wounded and missing, is 357.[14] It is estimated that about 70 of the wounded will be again fit for service.

J. H. G.

P.S.—Two more monitors arrived this afternoon, ready to take a part in the combat. The men of the regiment are raising a sum to send the body of the Colonel home, as soon as Fort Wagner is reduced. They all declare that they will dig for his body till they find it. They are determined this disgrace shall be counteracted by something noble.[15]

12. Captains Cabot Jackson Russel and William H. Simpkins were both from Boston, as were many of the 54th's officers. Col. E. N. Hallowell's official report submitted to Brig. Gen. Truman Seymour on Nov. 7, 1863, lists them as missing, presumed killed. Eleven other officers of the regiment, including Colonel Hallowell, were wounded. The temporary appointment of Col. Milton S. Littlefield from the 4th South Carolina (Colored), whose own regiment had too few men to remain in service, was not popular in the regiment or in Massachusetts (Emilio, *History of the Fifty-fourth,* 90–91, 107).

13. Emilio described the exceptional difficulties presented by the terrain—narrow causeways, swamps, and streams bridged for long distances with one or two planks on pilings, and no handrails. On the night of the evacuation, driving rain, planks slippery with muck, and intense darkness punctuated by occasional flashes of lightning compounded the problems (ibid., 64–65).

14. This figure is probably a typographical error. Colonel Hallowell's report records 9 killed, 147 wounded and 100 missing, for a total of 256 casualties among the enlisted men, plus 14 casualties in the officer ranks (ibid., 90–91).

15. *Nantucket* went into action July 24, and *Passaic* rejoined the fleet on July 25 (Hunter, *Year on a Monitor,* 109). On Aug. 24, 1863, Shaw's father wrote to General

[*Mercury*, August 5, 1863]

Our correspondent, "J.H.G." is a member of Co. C., of the 54th Massachusetts regiment. He is a colored man, belonging to this city, and his letters are printed by us, *verbatim et literatim*, as we receive them. He is a truthful and intelligent correspondent, and a good soldier. [*Mercury* Editor]

Gillmore requesting that no further efforts be made to recover his son's body, saying "We hold that a soldier's most appropriate burial-place is on the field where he has fallen" (quoted in Emilio, *History of the Fifty-fourth*, 103–4).

4

Yankee Pandemonium
Charleston, South Carolina, August and September 1863

After two unsuccessful frontal attacks on Fort Wagner in which he lost one-third of his men, General Gillmore was ready to try a different approach. He would lay siege to the fort, constructing trenches, or saps, which could bring his heavy guns ever closer to the enemy's batteries. The first parallel was begun 1,350 yards from Wagner on July 23. One month later the fifth parallel had been completed within 200 yards of the fort.

The work was carried out under incredibly difficult conditions. The heat was almost unbearable; moving the heavy guns and setting them up on shifting sand or marsh mud required extraordinary strength and engineering skill; and with little natural cover for protection, workers at the front were frequent victims of rebel sharpshooters.

By mid-August the advancing parallels had brought Fort Sumter well within reach of Union artillery and it was decided not to wait for the fall of Wagner before attempting Sumter's destruction. Therefore on August 17 the Morris Island batteries, joined by the ironclads, began an intense bombardment of the fort which continued without letup for seven days. At the end of that time Fort Sumter was, in General Gillmore's words, "a shapeless and harmless mass of ruins,"[1] yet it steadfastly refused to surrender. General Gillmore now expected the fleet to proceed into Charleston Harbor. Admiral Dahlgren and the Navy Department evidently thought it still too risky and the fleet stayed

1. *ORA* 1, 28.1: 3.

put. Meanwhile the army continued moving toward Fort Wagner. In early September, aided by
a bombardment from the land batteries and offshore fleet, the advance work party was within 100
yards of the fort.

Preparations were made for the
final assault to take place on the
morning of September 7, but the
battle plan was not needed. Gen-

eral Beauregard, recognizing that
his weakened force could hold out
no longer, had ordered the evacuation of the fort on the previous
evening. When Union troops entered next morning they found no
one there. By the end of the day all
Morris Island from Lighthouse Inlet to Cumming's Point was in
Union hands.

[*Mercury*, August 16, 1863]

Morris Island, August 3, 1863

Messrs. Editors:—The latest news from this department is the capture of a blockade runner having on board heavy Whitworth guns. The
guns captured are now in course of erection on the north end of the
Island to bombard the fort, which they were intended to defend. The
planting of siege guns steadily progresses, but is necessarily slow, as
the guns have to be hauled through a marsh, and that too in the night,
so the enemy cannot see what we are about, and to avert their constant
rain of shells, they thinking of course we can't work when they are
shelling us; but they may find out their mistake before this week is out.
Every available man on the Island is constantly at work, so as to bring
things to a speedy issue. Some are throwing up breastworks, some
hauling guns, others loading shells, or carting ammunition from the
wharf to the magazines, and every one is confident of success, helping
cheerfully in the great amount of work, which must be done before the
"grand ball" comes off. It is evident the Commanding General intends
to make a sure thing of it this time, and not make the assault till he has
got everything ready. One noticeable feature is Gen. Gillmore is super-
vising the preparations himself, and I do not think any man in the
department works more than he does. The consequence is the men has
confidence in him, and the rebels a corresponding degree of fear of the

"intrepid engineer," as they term him. As I write, the rebels are vainly blazing away, while our men both white and black are steadily pursuing their work right in their very teeth. When they see the flash from Fort Sumter they merely slip into their caves, dug already for the purpose, and after the shell has exploded, out they come and go to work again, till old Sumter gives them another salute. I have been up to the front three times this week, but "I still live," and all the others who have been up there.

The rebels are evidently getting scared. Last Tuesday we could see a balloon hovering over Charleston for over an hour; they were doubtless reconnoitering, but I think it is likely they could see they would be warmly received, should they take a notion to visit us. We were enlightened by the New York or Boston press, of the 18th to 20th ult. We were informed that the Monitors had reduced Forts Wagner and Sumter on the 11th, and Beauregard had evacuated and burned Charleston! And another yarn, of two regiments planting a flag on Fort Wagner, and holding it two hours! which would have been, but for the cowardice of a Pennsylvania regiment—all of which stories are sells, and must be compared with the Commanding General's official report. The fact is, "our own special correspondents travelling with Gen. So-and-so's division" are a good deal like the "highly intelligent contraband," or the "gentleman of undoubted veracity"—they write of what they hear, rather than what they see. In a conversation with one of the men of the 6th Conn. regiment, which was in the charge first made, he said if any one got in the fort it was more than he knew, and he said the regiment which had been mentioned as acting cowardly had been wronged.

There is one name I omitted in the two last letters. Nathan L. Young of New Bedford, was wounded on the night of the 18th, and died on board the steamer before arriving at Hilton Head. According to Lieut. Grace's official report from the Surgeon General at Beaufort, Corp. Torrance is not there, and the men who have arrived from there corroborate the statement. So he is among the killed or prisoners, as I intimated in my first letter. I am unable to give you any account of how the wounded are getting along, as I have received no communication from any of them since they have been there. Our boys have got over their depression of spirit somewhat, caused by the fall of so many of their companions, in the dawning of a speedy victory. They are all in hopes of another "good time" before going into Charleston, but they would a *leetle* rather have it on a fair field, with no odds. Charging is good when you have a fair sight; but they all agree that Wagner is a hot place.

J. H. G.

[*Mercury*, August 21, 1863]

Morris Island, Aug. 9, 1863

Messrs. Editors:—Since my last weekly melange, the situation remains about the same in this department. The 55th regiment, Col. N. P. Hallowell commanding, arrived here from Newbern last Monday, and on Tuesday the regiment was introduced to Messrs. Shovel and Spade, a firm largely interested in building rifle pits, breastworks and batteries. The men appear to be in splendid physical condition, and take the two regiments in the aggregrate, I think the 55th is superior in material to the 54th. But the hardships incident to a soldier's life may equalize them in a month or two.[2]

Last Wednesday night, as a party of men on a fatigue expedition were approaching Fort Johnson, a little too near, they narrowly escaped being captured. The party were in boats containing lumber, for the purpose of building a bridge across the creek which divides this island from James Island. The tide falling, near morning they were discovered by the rebel pickets, who commenced firing on them. Had not our own sharpshooters been near, the rebels would no doubt have captured some of our men; as it was, however, the fatigue party scrambled out of the boats, and made tracks through the mud and mire for camp. The rebels did succeed in capturing a captain and five men, but they escaped.

The sickly season has now about commenced; daily we hear the muffled drum, accompanied by the shrill, shrieking tones of the fife,

2. Norwood Penrose Hallowell was the younger brother of Col. Edward N. Hallowell, on sick leave as commander of the 54th. The Massachusetts 55th Regiment began organizing at Readville on May 12 from the overflow of recruits for the 54th. The regiment left Boston for the South on July 21 without having heard of the gallant assault on Fort Wagner (ibid., 329, 8).

which tells us that the "fell destroyer, Death," is near. Three times yesterday the plaintive notes of Bonaparte crossing the Alps were played passing our camp, followed by some noble son of New England in each instance. Our own regiment, too, lost one yesterday. His name was John Pieere, of Philadelphia; his complaint was fever.[3]

About noon yesterday there was sudden cessation of firing; the cause of it was the rebels sent out a flag of truce, and after that some of the general officers rode to the front and met those bearing it. What the result was is not known; but there were many rumors afloat during the afternoon in regard to it; some even hinting that Fort Wagner's defenders wished to sue for conditional terms; others to the effect that the "populace" of Charleston, not unlike their confreres in New York, were becoming clamorous for peace, threatening Jeff, Beauregard & Co. with violence if they persisted in holding on to Charleston, in view of the vast preparations the "Yankees" were making for their destruction; and that Beauregard came to make some treaty for the surrender of the city. But the news manufacturers didn't hit the nail on the head, I guess, for by 6 o'clock they were blazing away at each other nicely, with every prospect of—"to be continued."

Last Wednesday afternoon the companies were all formed in line in their respective streets, when Col. Littlefield addressed each company separately to this effect: "I have been requested by the paymaster to say that if the men are ready to receive TEN dollars per month as part pay, he will come over and pay the men off; you need not be afraid though that you won't get your THIRTEEN dollars per month, for you surely will." He then went on explaining how this little financial hitch was brought about, by telling us of some old record on file in relation to paying laborers or contrabands employed on public works, which the War Department had construed as applying to colored soldiers, urging us to take the TEN NOW and wait for some action of the Government for the other three. He then said, "all who wish to take the ten dollars per month, raise your right hand," and I am glad to say not one man in the whole regiment lifted a hand. He then said, we might not receive any

3. John W. Peer, aged twenty-one, Company B, was a barber from Philadelphia. He died of dysentery. Emilio reports that from July 18 to August 1 no rain fell and the heat was terrible. On the latter date 1,900 men were reported sick in camp (ibid., 347, 108).

money till after the convening of Congress. We replied that we had been over five months waiting, and we would wait till the Government could frame some special law, for the payment of part of its troops. The 2d South Carolina regiment was paid the ten dollars per month; but we were enlisted under different circumstances. Too many of our comrades' bones lie bleaching near the walls of Fort Wagner to subtract even one cent from our hard earned pay. If the nation can ill afford to pay us, we are men and will do our duty while we are here without a murmur, as we have done always, before and since that day we were offered to sell our manhood for ten dollars per month.[4]

J. H. G.

P.S.—I have just learned on "undoubted authority" that the flag of truce was for the purpose of returning the letters, valuables and money found on our dead and wounded in the assault of the 18th July. This may seem wonderful, that the rebels should act so honorably, but it is a fact. May be they are putting in practice what Hon. A. H. Stephens undertook to negotiate, thinking we will be magnanimous when we enter Charleston.[5]

J. H. G.

[*Mercury,* August 29, 1863]

Morris Island, Aug. 16, 1863

Messrs. Editors:—As stringent orders have been recently issued relative to giving information in regard to military matters here, which is a very proper course and necessary, the amount of news is rather meagre, so I will violate no "General Orders"[6] in expressing the general feeling of the regiment in respect to our late commander, Col.

---

4. For a summary of the pay issue see Appendix A.

5. Alexander Hamilton Stephens, vice-president of the Confederacy, had been trying to open negotiations to regularize the exchange of prisoners of war.

6. General Orders No. 66, issued Aug. 7, 1863: "The practice of giving information to their friends or to the public press, on matters concerned with military operations in progress or in contemplation . . . must be stopped at once. No information which could in any way benefit the enemy must be divulged, directly or indirectly. . . . By order of Brig. Gen. Q. A. Gillmore" (*ORA* 1, 28.2: 40).

Robert G. Shaw. Now that he is no more with us, the men appreciate his qualities, as a friend, commander and hero, and, I might add, without any extravagance, a martyr—for such he has proved himself to be. Who would dare ascribe a selfish motive to a man whose position in life bade fair to be a high one, without the prestige of military fame? He seemed to have taken the position more in the light of a reformer, or one to put in practice a system of order and discipline among a people sadly deficient in these respects, not in a military sense alone, because the seed of discipline sown among us as soldiers would ripen into fruit when the time arrived to become citizens. We, as a people, would know the value of obedience and the meaning of law and order; but I am off the point. When the raising of this regiment was first mooted I doubt if there could have been found a dozen men in the North, holding as high a position and with prospects of bettering themselves by another channel, as our respected Colonel, who would have accepted the unenviable position as commander of the first colored regiment organized in the North. There was then a great doubt among skeptical persons of our raising 500 men; and doubts, too, of colored men conforming to the restraint of camp life, and predictions that the men would run away in a week after being brought to camp; with these doubts and predictions before them, men were afraid to risk their reputations and name on what too many deemed a chimera; they did not care to stand a chance of being the laughing stock and butt of cynical persons. But Col. Shaw, from the beginning, never evinced any fear of what others thought or said. He believed the work would be done, and he put his hands, his head, and heart to the task, with what results you all know. It has been conceded by many that he carried through Boston one of the best drilled regiments ever raised by the State. The discipline of the regiment was perfect; not a slavish fear, but obedience enacted by the evidence of a superior and directing mind.

Col. Shaw was not what might be expected, familiar with his men; he was cold, distant, and even austere, to a casual observer. When in the line of duty, he differed totally from what many persons would suppose he would be, as commander of a negro regiment. If there was any abolition fanaticism in him, he had a mind well balanced, so that no man in the regiment would ever presume to take advantage of that feeling in their favor, to disobey, or use insolence; but had any man a wrong done him, in Colonel Shaw he always found an impartial judge, providing the complaint was presented through the proper channels. For he was very formal in all his proceedings, and would enforce obedience merely by his tones which were not harsh, but soft and firm. The last day with us, or I may say the ending of it, as we lay flat on the ground before the assault, his manner was more unbending[7] than I had ever noticed before in the presence of his men; he sat on the ground, and was talking to the men very familiarly and kindly; he told them how the eyes of thousands would look upon the night's work they were about to enter on; and said he, "Now boys I want you to be MEN!" He would walk along the entire line and speak words of cheer to his men. We could see that he was a man who had counted the cost of the undertaking before him, for his words were spoken so ominously, his lips were compressed, and now and then there was visible a slight twitching of the corners of his mouth, like one bent on accomplishing or dying.[8] One poor fellow, struck no doubt by the Colonel's determined bearing, exclaimed as he was passing him, "Colonel, I will stay by you till I die," and he kept his word; he has never been seen since. For one so young, Col. Shaw showed a well-trained mind, and an ability of governing men not possessed by many older and more experienced men. In him, the regiment has lost one of its best and most devoted friends. Requiescat in pace.

J. H. G.

[*Mercury*, September 7, 1863]

Morris Island, Aug. 23, 1863

Messrs. Editors:—Supposing a detailed account of the operations now in progress in this quarter would prove interesting to your readers, I have taken the pains to jot them down as they occur, trusting to the leniency of the commanding officer to let the MSS. pass. On Monday morning, the 17th, the bombardment commenced. Such a roar of heavy cannon I greatly doubt has been heard since the art of war has been

7. I.e., unbent, relaxed.
8. Shaw apparently had a strong premonition of his own death, which he twice expressed to Colonel Hallowell in the days before the assault on Wagner (Emilio, *History of the Fifty-fourth*, 62, 67).

known; for the heaviest guns ever cast in the known world are now banging away at the doomed citadels of rebellion, Forts Wagner and Sumter. Shot after shot tears up the bricks and mortar of Sumter's walls, but still her flag floats defiantly from the battlement. Battery Gregg, a little to the right of Sumter, has been silent the greater part of the day, as the rains of the Yankee Pandemonium are a little too hot for such small fry as herself. The clouds of sand which anon rise up around Fort Wagner give the surest indication that our gallant artillerists are unerring marksmen. To give you any information concerning the number, kind or position of guns would be violating a strict and necessary order; but suffice it to say that the work goes on in a manner assuring success. Slow, but sure, is the policy evidently pursued now, and it is fair to anticipate the fall of secession's mother before the genial days of September are gone.

At evening, after the first day's work, the firing ceased on the side of the rebels, and it being very dark and hazy, our side ceased also, with the exception of a shell now and then, probably to let the rebels know that folks were awake this side of Sumter. The next morning the ball re-opened with renewed vigor and Sumter now began to show symptoms of rough usage. The mortar schooners keep up a slow shelling of Wagner,[9] but from the look of things, the navy appear at present to hold faith in the poet's line, "Distance lends enchantment to the view." There was one casualty this day; one man of the 3d R.I. battery was almost instantly killed by a fragment of shell. On Wednesday the siege was progressing the same as the two days previous, with a steady diminution in the height and architectural beauty of the walls of Sumter and the regularity of the lines of Wagner's parapet. Thursday morning; again the contending guns are belching forth their sheets of flame, reminding us that these are war times. The rebels are very active this morning, if judged by the number of shells they are throwing so promiscuously over the north end of the island; but these do not appear to scare Gen. Gillmore; he means to go ahead, and go he will. Friday may be considered about the same as the days preceding it, and we expect it will continue so for some time yet, though the rebels are evidently hard

9. These small sailing vessels each carried a short-barreled cannon with low muzzle velocity that could lob shells in a high trajectory.

pushed, when judged by their slow fire from Wagner and Sumter, indicating scant resources in ammunition, at least, if not in provisions.

There was a very impressive cortege passed by our camp this morning, which is one of the inevitable concomitants of soldier life. There is a queer mixture of joy and sorrow in an army. Lieut. Holbrook, of the 3d R.I. battery, was followed to his last resting place by a detachment of his regiment, a large number of officers and a company of infantry, with two field pieces, escorted by the band of the 6th Conn. regiment. Lieut. Holbrook was a Massachusetts officer, and formerly was one of the 10th Mass. battery. He was struck by a piece of shell while training a gun, of which he was in charge. He lingered two days in the most intense agony. He was an officer beloved and respected both by his fellow officers and men, and his death is one more sacrifice, on the altar of freedom, of a brave and patriotic son of New England.

J. H. G.

[*Mercury,* September 15, 1863]

Morris Island, Aug. 30, 1863

Messrs. Editors:—The past week has developed nothing very stirring that I am aware of, though there may be a number of manufactured "tales" in the mail gleanings, or "the very latest by telegraph." But for the information of those who feel anxious, I will merely state that Morris Island is bounded on one side by the Atlantic Ocean, and a number of bogs and quagmires on another, and last, though not least, by numerous rebel guns on "tother side." Of course the siege is progressing finely; how could it be otherwise? For don't you all know that Charleston was to have fallen the next day surely, for the last month and more! (Vide New York Herald.) Query. What has become of the barque Growler, cleared from Boston with a cargo of "cooling material for Charleston Bar"? This hot weather makes us feel solicitous for her safety. We fear something awful has happened, such a sad casualty perhaps as the ice melting away—in tumblers sitting on high official tables.

Last Thursday night our pickets were successful in assaulting and carrying the rebel rifle pits, close under Wagner, say within 270 yards.

Among the captured prisoners, amounting in all to 63, are 5 black men; two were fully armed and equipped, as REBEL SHARPSHOOTERS. They had the very best pattern of rifle, "neutral" make, and are represented by the "trash" as unerring shots. The other three were at work in the trenches. One of these sable rebels is represented to be a reb at <u>heart</u>; he is a large owner of chattels himself, and does not seem to exhibit any of that humble or cowering mien, to indicate that he thinks himself inferior to the "Great Jeff" himself. He holds himself aloof from the other "misguided brethren," the same as my Lord of the olden time did from his vassals. There may be many more such men as that in the South; but the idea of Mr. Davis relying on his attached and docile SERVANTS to recuperate his wasted armies is all moonshine. In the first place HE knows better than to try any such experiment. The slaves would very likely be glad to get arms, but Mr. Davis probably is certain they would USE them on the "kind and indulgent upholders of the peculiar institution" instead of the "marauding Yankees." And if he takes the chattels to fill the army, who is to raise the "wittles?" Patriotism and dreams of a Great Southern Empire may sustain the SPIRIT of treason, but the rebels are not Joves nor wizards; they must eat. But I hope Mr. Davis may so far forget himself as to call on every able negro in his so called Confederacy, for it is plain to be seen that they would only be ready to fall into Uncle Sam's ranks at the first opportunity, with the advantage of coming to us armed and equipped, at the expense of the Confederacy, and—"Neutral Britain."

Last Sunday we had a grand review of troops. The 54th was the only colored regiment in the column, sandwiched between the white troops. No one on the ground seemed to perceive any signs of danger arising from such close proximity. The regiment was highly complimented by the Commanding General on its cleanliness of dress, good conduct and proficiency in drill. So you see the 54th is bound to live down all prejudice against its color, by a determination to do well in any position it is put. If it is to wield the shovel and pick, do it faithfully; if it is to haul siege guns, or load and unload transports, our motto is, work faithfully and willingly. The regiment has been on guard and picket very little since coming here, as it gained a reputation of being a good working regiment; so we have been pretty well worked out for the last month, but the most of us are yet living.

J. H. G.

Morris Island, Sept. 5, 1863

Messrs. Editors:—As there is nothing to record the past week, other than the (insignificant?) death of a dozen pickets, or as many more laborers in trenches, of course you must expect a dull letter. We had hoped the weather would continue cool, as it had been the last week, but the thermometer is now up to the old numbers, 112 to 98; but the nights are very chilly. We have been so unfortunate as to lose three men during the week, who were at work at the front, besides five severely wounded. One of the men killed, George King, last place of residence, Toledo, Ohio, was once a slave, belonging to Gen. [John Cabell] Breckinridge, rebel army, and his mother and one sister are yet slaves, now in Richmond, Va. The others killed were Alexander Vanderpoel, of Coxsackie, N.Y. and Geo. Hunter, of Cleveland, O.[10] It is now an ordinary spectacle to see stretchers passing, with blood trickling through the canvass, with some poor fellow who was wounded on picket or assisting the engineers. That is the last we ever hear or know of it; they are borne to the grave, and all the news-devouring people think is, "Oh that's nothing, why don't they have a great big battle, so we shall have a respectable list of killed, mangled and missing?" But the relatives and friends of the patriot soldier who is killed or wounded by a chance fragment of a shell, or a sharpshooter's deadly aim, are apt to feel as bad as though the victim died on the ramparts, waving a battle flag before an assaulting column. A man dies none the less gloriously, standing at his post on picket, or digging in the trench; his country needs him there, and he is as true a soldier as though he were in the thickest fray.[11] We should like to know from the North how the siege is progressing; we are pretty close to the work, but we know nothing as regards the news.

10. Toward the end of August, the 54th was sent to relieve the 3rd U.S. Colored Troops in the advance trenches. King was of Company K, the others belonged to Company H. Hunter actually survived his wounds and was discharged in June 1864 (Emilio, *History of the Fifty-fourth*, 375).

11. By this time the front had advanced beyond any natural cover, and enemy fire more frequently found victims among the fatigue details and pickets working there. From August 19 to September 3 the three guard regiments at the front lost 10 percent of their whole force, mainly from artillery fire. Deaths from shelling, as well as from disease in camp, were so numerous during this period, and funeral music so constant, that orders were finally issued to ban the music, as being too depressing for the men (ibid., 119, 116).

I saw one of our boys brushing his dress-coat very carefully the other day, and asked him what he was so particular for. He said he wanted to have his clothes look nice, because he "guessed we would soon march into Charleston!" Of course, I hope he will be gratified in his wish, and do not doubt him in the main, if he will ignore "soon." It is pretty generally believed that Sumter is evacuated, for it does not seem possible for men to stay in it, in its present dilapidated condition. There appears to be no signs of work going on in the fort, neither has there been a gun fired these three weeks from her. But there are "other fish to fry" besides Sumter, and you may depend upon it that they will be done brown by the fire the Chef de Cuisine will put under them. Time works wonders, and time is needed to take Charleston.

Monitor

[*Mercury*, September 21, 1863]

Morris Island, Sept. 9, 1863

Messrs. Editors:—At last Wagner and Gregg have the old flag waving over them. Sumter is a mass of shapeless ruins; Gregg is occupied by our forces, a small detachment of men, to repair and hold it. The agreeable fact was doubted a long time this morning by those whose duties were otherwheres but the "front." But by sunrise, all doubts were cleared by the evidence of prisoners and trophies. The attack was made about 2 1-2 o'clock this morning by Generals Terry and Stevenson, and in half an hour the welkin rang with the loud cheers of our victorious army. While one part of our force were taking possession of Wagner, another small detachment marched on battery Gregg; but the rebels, panic-stricken by flying fugitives from Wagner, commenced to follow. So by one well-directed blow, we have swept the rebels from their strongest positions for the defence of Charleston. This is emphatically a triumph of skill; repulsed twice with a great loss of life, the Commanding General has at last been successful in proving the oft boasted impregnability of the defences of Charleston to be all moonshine in the age of science and expedients. Gen. Gillmore can proudly say he has gained what the rebels most dreaded to lose, without the loss of hardly a life. To be sure life has been sacrificed in the preparations to accomplish the great end; for how could it be otherwise, when the work had to be done under a heavy fire, and a continuous rain of shell, grape, and canister. Indeed what seemed to be the preliminary of a grand coup de main, was in fact the work which scared the rebels out. The bombardment commenced at daylight, Sept. 5th, and was kept up without intermission till Sunday night at 11 1-2 o'clock by the land batteries, and Ironsides, and "cheese boxes."[12] No wonder Wagner fell! Such a continuous pour of shot and shell never struck one work so accurately and effectively as on Saturday and Sunday; our trenches then being so close to the parapet of Wagner that the recoil of pieces of shell from our own guns wounded our men, who were digging the "last parallel," that our boys could have a covered way to enter Wagner. All hands are satisfied, one with the other, and all feel that they are well repaid for disappointments and toil, and that each and every man reflect[s] credit and glory on the old flag, which waves defiantly at the gates of rebeldom. I have not room to describe the infernal machines put in the way by the rebels to destroy our men; suffice it to say, these torpedoes have killed many of our men when struck by them with their spades. In the trenches they had another diabolical contrivance consisting of a hook, not unlike a "gaff" (used by whalemen in handling blubber), and a lance with a long shank, the point of the lance being about 9 inches from the hook. These are mounted on poles five or six feet long and were no doubt purposely made for spearing men when charging, and then pulling them in the fort with the hooks. I was in the work a short time today, but could not stay long enough to gain any correct idea of how it is arranged internally; the sand is piled up in huge heaps here and there, almost completely covering the entrance to the bomb-proofs. There is nothing evidently in its appearance now to give one a just appreciation of the engineering displayed in its construction. I have not been so far

12. Between sixty and seventy guns and mortars from land batteries and the naval squadron were trained on Wagner and Gregg, firing almost 4,000 shots in forty-two hours (John Johnson, *The Defense of Charleston Harbor* [New York, 1889], quoted in Hunter, *Year on a Monitor*, 126). The *New Ironsides*, named for the sailing frigate *Constitution* known as "Old Ironsides," was an armored auxiliary steam frigate, ship-rigged, of 3,486 tons, and carrying fourteen smoothbores and two Parrott rifles. She had formerly served as Admiral DuPont's flagship. The shape of the monitor—a low, flat hull with a single turret on the deck—caused these vessels to be called cheese-boxes on rafts.

as Gregg or Sumter yet and if they smell as bad as Wagner, I don't want to. The smell in Wagner is really sickening, dead men and mules are profuse, some exposed to the rays of sun, and others being half buried by earth thrown over them by our shot and shell during the bombardment. Forts Moultrie and Johnson are now vainly trying to make the "Yankee" leave Wagner, but the monitors bark at them every now and then, so they will soon be silent.

Killed Sept. 5th by our own guns—Charles Van Allen, of Lenox, Mass., and Aaron Spencer, of North Lee, Mass., both of Co. A, 54th Mass. regiment.

Yours truly

Monitor

5

A Monotonous State of Affairs
Charleston, South Carolina, September and October 1863

The fierce bombardment of Fort Sumter at the end of August had reduced its fire power to one gun, which faced up harbor. Independent of each other General Gillmore and Admiral Dahlgren determined to storm the fort. On the night of September 8 the admiral despatched a naval force of nineteen officers and some 400 sailors and marines in thirty boats, but the Confederates were prepared and the walls of the fort were impossible to scale. The assault was a complete failure, leaving three men killed and 104 taken prisoner. *General Gillmore's expedition, meanwhile, had been delayed by the tide and was subsequently aborted.*

After this, tension between the two commanders increased. General Gillmore believed that "the capture of all of Morris Island and the demolition of Fort Sumter completed those portions of the plan of joint operations against the defenses of Charleston in which the land forces were to take the lead."[1] As far as he was concerned, it was now up to the navy to move aggressively on Charleston.

[*Mercury*, October 1, 1863]

Morris Island, Sept. 19, 1863

Messrs. Editors:—"All quiet" in this department of the South is a very appropriate mode of expressing the operations the past week with

1. *ORA* 1, 28.1: 28.

us here. Although you may expect at no distant day to hear of stirring actions, that is, if signalizing, backing up and backing down mean anything. The monitors run up—fall in line—up goes a signal from the flag vessel—they break ranks, and, blow off steam out of gun range of old Moultrie. A comical chap in our company says, he guesses "they are having dress parade." We expected to see the cheese boxes knock Sullivan's Island batteries higher than a kite long ago, but we are agreeably left to keep expecting.[2] But the land forces are busy preparing for something, but what it is to be I can't venture to say for fear it may prove greatly the reverse. But if I were a rebel, and lived in Charleston, I should feel decidedly skittish to see the villainous Yankees planting those dangerous Parrot guns right in front of the city, and less than 4 miles off too.[3] Mr. Beauregard is aware that those barbarous engines of war will carry a message a little over five miles. Hence his persistent efforts to shell us out of Wagner and Gregg. The mathematician of the regiment estimates that if the number of shells wasted by old Beaury costs three dollars in good money, it will only take three months and seven days to run out the last Confederate loan—each shell costing $15 in rebel scrip. I think Senator Toombs should point out the utter folly and extravagance of Beauregard's course, as the Senator is deeply concerned about the Confederate finances.[4]

Night and day the rebels are pouring shell around Wagner, Gregg, and on our camps on Black Island, or at the "Swamp Angel"[5] but so far,

2. Battery Bee and Battery Beauregard supplemented the fire power of Fort Moultrie from Sullivan's Island.

3. Named for their inventor, Robert P. Parrott, these rifled guns were first produced in 1860. They had a reinforcing band around the breech which allowed the gun to fire heavier charges than had previously been possible. After Union troops gained control of Morris Island, General Gillmore set up new batteries on Cumming's Point with the guns trained on Charleston (Chaitin, *Coastal War*, 139).

4. Robert Toombs, United States representative and senator from Georgia before the war, served in the Confederate Provisional Congress and as Confederate secretary of state.

5. The "Swamp Angel" was an eight-inch, 200-pound Parrott gun trained on Charleston, a distance of about 8,800 yards from its battery of the same name which was located in a marsh between James and Morris islands. The gun was first fired on August 20 but burst on the thirty-sixth round and was replaced with two mortars (Emilio, *History of the Fifty-fourth*, 108, 112, 114, 225; Hunter, *Year on a Monitor*, 122–23).

they would have accomplished as much had they fired at the moon. Yesterday, they appeared to be unusually extravagant—from the north end of James Island all the way down to Seceshville, they kept their batteries open (numbering 12 guns), firing at—nobody knows; it is certain their shot came no where near Morris Island. It is said a magazine was blown up on James Island last Tuesday, but I cannot rely upon it; there certainly was a great smoke seen over there, but it might have been a fire in the woods.[6] Of course, every rebel magazine blown up is considered a gain to the Union cause, in the same light of the "utter demoralization" of such and such a rebel army, or a "strong Union sentiment" existing in this or that section, and many persons are credulous enough to believe that all such natural combinations will end the war, instead of good hard fighting. The best mode of creating Union sentiments now, is by planting artillery near the thresholds of those who are without them, and if you get that close to them, you must fight hard to get there; that is, you will have to demoralize the army between you and the apocryphal Union section by giving them a good sound drubbing, or else capture and put them in the penitentiary.

We had a heavy gale here, lasting all day Wednesday and Thursday; the rain came down as it only can in these latitudes, with a vengeance. The most of the shipping inside the bar had to be towed out, for fear some of them would be swept ashore. The beach was strewn with boats, broke loose from vessels in the offing, stumps of huge trees, timber and spars. I saw the floor ribs of a good-sized ship high and dry on the beach, drove up by the fury of the waves. She may be a relic of the stone blockade, as I saw a piece of a vessel's knighthead marked "Corea," and I believe there was a ship of that name in the stone fleet.[7] The

6. "On the 15th [of September] the enemy's magazine in the latter work [Battery Cheves] was accidentally blown up with 1,200 pounds of powder. . . . The force of this explosion was felt all over Morris Island" (Emilio, *History of the Fifty-fourth*, 129).

7. *Corea*, a New London whaleship, was part of Stone Fleet No. 1, the sixteen stone-laden vessels sent from the North in December 1861 to be sunk across Charleston's main channel in order to obstruct shipping. However, *Corea* was turned over to the army quartermaster at Port Royal for a storeship. The ship *Courier*, which in Yankee dialect might sound the same, was among the vessels sunk (Arthur Gordon, "The Great Stone Fleet: Calculated Catastrophe," *United States Naval Institute Proceedings* 94, no. 12 [1968]: 78). In large wooden vessels the knighthead consisted of the upper ends of the

weather is quite cool here since the storm; it is very comfortable in the day time, but the nights make an overcoat indispensable. I believe the bark Growler, or Grumbler, has arrived at last. Misfortunes or blessings never come singly—now we have cold weather, we have ice water. But the soldiers thank the donors all the same, and bless the good people who thought of them weeks ago, when the days were long and sultry.

As I have taken too much of your space, I will end by giving the thanks of the 54th regiment to their friends in the Sperm City for the interest taken in our behalf. May they ever have plenty of "spondulicks" to relieve the boys in the field, if they can't relieve us on picket.[8]

Monitor

[*Mercury*, October 8, 1863]

Morris Island, Sept. 26, 1863

Messrs. Editors:—Since my last epistle to the "elect in Bedford," there has nothing very eventful transpired. How long we are doomed to this monotonous state of affairs, I can't presume to say; the army has done about all in its power to do in this mode of attack on Charleston and are now putting the captured works in a state of defence. Whether it is the intention to inaugurate any further offensive operations from Gregg or Wagner seems to be uncertain. One thing has been clearly demonstrated in this campaign. It is almost useless to undertake to drive an enemy out of sand works at long range. We have tried it on the rebels, and they in turn have tried it on us, with about the same effect. Sand works will stand too, a close bombardment, unless you pitch shell right into them; so if the approaches to Charleston are to be taken before the city lies at our mercy, it will be necessary to bring the iron fleet to close

---

foremost framing timbers into which the bowsprit was set. The timbers were often extended with ornamental carvings.

8. New Bedford, the world's greatest whaling port, derived much of its wealth from the products of the sperm whale. "Spondulicks," meaning money or cash, came into slang usage in the United States about 1857 (Eric Partridge, *A Dictionary of Slang and Unconventional English* [London, 1949], 813).

quarters. If there is not enough of them, send for more; for the more vessels we have engaged, the worse for the rebels. The monitors and iron boats were expected to revolutionize naval warfare radically. We have boastingly intimated that the strongest fortified cities were no longer a bugbear and scare to our invulnerable fleets; but we have yet to hear of one stronghold on the sea, or gulf coasts at least, laid low by their prowess.[9] I believe the iron fleet is all that is claimed for it. But we don't expect the monitors to go up Charleston harbor of themselves. We want a Nelson or Perry, or some one like the Commodore who was determined to "go up to New Orleans, or sink every ship he had."[10] When we have some one of that stamp we may expect to see Charleston fall, or else by the long and tedious mode of mapping them out, by way of James or Sullivan's Islands. The first cry was, Fort Sumter is in the way; —now, Fort Sumter is worse than useless, so far as being a defence to the city is concerned. But still the "Webb-feet" are holding on—to their anchors. Then it was, if Forts Wagner and Gregg are put out of the way, then what: why move the fleet up a little nearer and look on the wharves of Charleston, see the boats land and put off for Sullivan's Island, within gun range of even the land batteries on our side, and the monitors lying right in the mouth of the harbor and letting the rebel boats run from one point to another, not three miles from them, without making an effort to cripple them. Of course they must wait for orders to fire, and if the "great ram" itself came down I suppose 'twould be the same way.

Whether the government has sagely considered the quotation from Vattel,[11] as interpreted by the Charleston Courier, remains to be seen.

---

9. After the success of the original *Monitor* against the C.S.S. *Virginia (Merrimack)* in Hampton Roads, Virginia, on March 9, 1862, the federal government ordered dozens of the new vessels built. Disappointingly, they proved remarkably unseaworthy—slow-moving and balky at the helm. The failure of the naval attack on Fort Sumter, on April 7, 1863, in which five of the eight attacking monitors were totally or partially disabled, demonstrated that they were vulnerable as well (Hunter, *Year on a Monitor,* 47–61).

10. David Glasgow Farragut led the successful naval expedition against New Orleans in early spring 1862.

11. Emerich de Vattel, Swiss philosopher and jurist, was the author of *Droit des gens, ou, principes de la loi naturelle appliques a la conduite et aux affaires des nations* (1758) translated in 1760 as *Law of Nations.* General Beauregard had cited Vattel earlier in

But I can't help thinking, as a great many others think, that if the government exhibits so much needless humanity in deference to Mons. Vattel's played out theories, compiled two centuries since, as to restrain Gen. Gillmore from laying the nest of treason in her unhallowed dust now that he has the opportunity, we deserve to be beaten.

Does any man suppose that if the rebels had batteries planted, for instance on Long Island, or any where near New York on the Jersey side, they would have any scruples about burning New York with Greek fire if it did not surrender?[12] Suppose the New Yorkers should say, "By the law of nations and all the standard authorities in such matters, you cannot burn or shell our city until you have reduced and passed Fort Hamilton, the floating batteries, and every battery and gun outside the city limits for three miles." I think the rebels would be pretty apt to say, we are after the city. We don't want your forts and batteries if we can get your city without them, and if you burn the city yourselves, why the forts are then practically useless. The treasure they were built to protect will be gone, and the forts will have to succumb in a short time, for the city will be no more a base of supply to them. That is about the position Charleston is in now, and we must see to it that the traitors shall learn the cost of warring against their country. What if the London Times does work itself into a fume, and call on the "whole civilized world to witness the inhuman barbarity of the Americans." Don't America belong to us? or at least that part which causes England so much anxiety. We have never lashed a rebel to a gun and blown him to pieces, however richly some of them have deserved it; neither have we banished a great warrior and sovereign to an almost desolate island, and left him to die with scarcely a friend to close his eyes. We treated Vallandigham better, who should have been ducked and gagged.[13]

---

protesting the destruction of private residences in Darien (Beauregard to Gillmore, Charleston, July 4, 1863, *ORA* 1, 28.2: 11–13).

12. "Greek fire" was a flammable composition packed in tin tubes which were then put into shells along with the powder. Although the rain of Greek fire on Charleston initially spread terror, it soon became apparent that the incendiary shells were not particularly reliable or effective (*ORA* 1, 28.1: 33; Chaitin, *Coastal War*, 137; Emilio, *History of the Fifty-fourth*, 145).

13. Clement Laird Vallandigham, a leader of the Peace Democrats, was found guilty of

The number of casualties have been very small the past week, when we consider the persistent fire from the rebels. Our men at work up at Gregg and Wagner are most frequently admonished to "cover" from Johnson, or "lie low" from Moultrie. The shell and shot come screaming through the air, as though thirsting for a victim; nearing the work they explode, scattering the fragments around, and the pieces hum and buzz like a shoal of maddened wasps. It sounds very inspiriting, providing you are in a position of comparative safety. But I notice that some men won't cover; the consequence is they soon have someone to do it for them.

Monitor

[*Mercury*, October 15, 1863]

Morris Island, Oct. 3, 1863

Messrs. Editors:—All quiet here, so far as war news is concerned. We hear of nothing to cause any great excitement around us, for we are so familiar with "bombs bursting in air," and shot whizzing through space, that it would be an item were it to cease. We have been pegging away at Sumter, a little every day during the week, more I presume to keep them from working than anything else. The rebels opened in a new place yesterday; the battery is a little to the right of Castle Pinckney,[14] but from the looks of the place it must be a floating battery. I was up in Wagner at the time, and from the way the shot came they must have a very superior gun. The shot came unexpectedly, as the sentinels on the lookout were not dreaming of a shot from that direction, their attention being directed to James Island's "barkers," and Fort Moultrie, and Batteries Bee and Beauregard. Suddenly, there came a noise through the air, like an Erie lightning-express train, —then a terrible explosion, and the pieces of a Brook's shell were falling pell mell into the

---

treasonable sympathies in May 1863. President Lincoln commuted his original sentence of imprisonment to banishment in the South, and Vallandigham eventually made his way to Ontario.

14. A rebel fortification on the island at the mouth of the Cooper River flowing into Charleston Harbor.

interior of the fort.[15] Luckily not a man was hurt, although they had no time to "kiver," as the Second S. Carolina boys express it. After that, we kept a lookout for that chap, and the rest of the afternoon he kept one end of the fatigue pretty busy covering. It is almost incredible how we manage to do so much work under such a heavy and constant fire. Wagner and Gregg are ours, but it takes about as much courage to hold them as it did to take them; and then to work on them and completely change them is something more than digging on a canal or railroad. But it is just this trait of 'keeping all you get' in the Yankee character which will eventually beat the rebels. We believe in good sound doctrine—for war at any rate—"keep all and get more."

The iron clads are flourishing. I believe they are being painted; though I hear they captured a blockade runner last night, or one of the rebel rams, which it is rumored was coming out to raise the blockade. I don't know if this be true, as I have had no chance of learning anything definite. But I know there was a grand pow-wow on the water last night about 11 o'clock, as the big guns were bellowing at a great rate, the flag vessel was signalizing rapidly, and taken altogether, I guess there was something of the ram kind or neutral traders around.

The subscriptions and collections towards the monument to Col. Robert G. Shaw have reached the sum of $1472, and it is proposed that the 54th contribute $1000. But we think the place proposed for its erection inexpedient, however much in keeping with poetic fitness. It is seriously proposed to erect it at the foot of Wagner's parapet, facing Fort Sumter. Now the manner and place where the hero fell will be known in history; a monument does not of necessity need to be placed where a hero fell; its place is some city or town, where people can see it. When we propose to erect a monument on some desolate island like this, it is simply creating a Mecca in the nineteenth century, where the race supposed to be benefited by the contest, which cost the hero his life, must make a toilsome pilgrimage in order to look upon it. We go in for the monument, but like not the idea of having it where, even when peace reigns supreme, it may be desecrated by unfriendly hands. They propose to erect a monument on soil which the enemies consider their

15. The shell came from a large-caliber rifled gun designed by John M. Brooke for the Confederacy.

own; and even should they be subjugated, which is stronger than conquered, it would ill become us to flaunt our success by raising monuments to our fallen heroes on their soil. Massachusetts is big enough to furnish a spot sufficient to honor one of her own soldiers; and I doubt not she would be very proud to have within her lines a monument of every son who has fallen in this trying war. We are ready to put in our mite, but we would rather see it raised on old Massachusetts soil. The first to say a black was a man, let her have the first monument raised by black men's money, upon her good old rocks.[16]

Monitor

[*Mercury*, October 20, 1863]

Morris Island, Oct. 10, 1863

Messrs. Editors:—The monotony of life was somewhat broken last Monday night, October 5th, by an insane attempt by the rebels to either capture or destroy the Ironsides. Their plans to destroy the vessel were to place torpedoes under her and blow her up. The attacking party came down out of the inner harbor about 9 o'clock, passed the two monitors lying between Gregg and Moultrie, hugging themselves in the belief that they were unseen.[17] But the ever watchful tars were very well aware of all the rebel manoeuvres. They let them go ahead, as it was the intention of the navy to trap the bold rascals. After the rebels had made the distance opposite the Ironsides, by running close along the beach of Sullivan's Island, they struck boldly, but cautiously, out for their prize. On they came, with muffled oars; but while they were approaching, the crew of the Ironsides were silently preparing to give their nocturnal (or

16. Others shared Gooding's point of view. The funds raised by the regiment were eventually used to found the first free school for Negro children in Charleston, named after Shaw. After the war, intermittent efforts were made to place a monument to Colonel Shaw in Boston, which finally resulted in the handsome memorial on Boston Common, designed by Augustus Saint-Gaudens and dedicated on May 31, 1897 (Richard Benson and Lincoln Kirstein, *Lay This Laurel* [New York, 1973]).

17. *David*, the attack vessel, was about fifty feet long, steam-powered, and shaped like a cigar. She rode low in the water and carried a crew of four. On the bow was mounted a contraption carrying a torpedo loaded with 100 pounds of rifle powder. For other accounts of the event see Hunter, *Year on a Monitor*, 140–44, and *ORN* 1, 15: 12–13.

infernal) visitors a warm reception. At length the rebel boats are within hailing distance—the marine on the bow of the Ironsides cries—"boat ahoy!" no response from the boats, but sudden and vigorous strokes with the oars, and shouts of, "pull hard! the Yankees are all turned in— we've got her sure—pull, pull, let's get aboard before they awake." A rocket from the Ironsides told the monitors to begin—out of their huge guns, they threw grape, cannister and shrapnel—the crew of the 'old invincible' mounted the railing and poured down a continual stream of minnie balls, which must have convinced the unlucky rebels that the Yankees were wide awake. Another nice little Yankee invention was used to advantage on this occasion; it is almost as nice as 'Greek Fire'; it is a contrivance to squirt steam. One party of rebels who were to place the torpedoes under the vessel, got out of range and pulled round to that side of the ships not in action, and got so close as to warrant them in throwing their infernals into the water, when lo! the skin-peeling element was in their midst! It is needless to say that they dropped their infernal machines, and intentions too. They could not stand such a novel mode of warfare as that, so they pulled for the nearest land under the control of Beaury—Sullivan's Island. I believe we did not take many prisoners, as the rebels decamped sooner than the officers supposed they would. We are waiting to hear another protest, or bull, by little "Peter," against squirting steam.[18]

While the navy was doing such active service, the land forces were all prepared and waiting for an invasion of the right little, tight little isle. There was no surety, but the rebels, by attracting all our attention to one point, would come like an avalanche on some other, as they agree that this island is their greatest loss. But they troubled us no more that night, nor will they be apt to for some time.

The attempt of the rebels to get possession of or destroy the Ironsides is pretty conclusive evidence that they admire her qualities as a fighting ram, or have a wholesome dread of her capacity to prove their obstructions all bosh. We shall no doubt be posted on her abilities that way soon, as matters appear to be coming to a point. Couriers ride, as if for dear life, bearing ponderous and ominous looking envelopes; some

18. Gen. Pierre (Peter) G. T. Beauregard had sent an angry despatch to General Gillmore after the August bombardment of Charleston calling it "an act of inexcusable barbarity" (Chaitin, *Coastal War*, 136).

look grave and reticent, others look cunning and knowing, like your London "cabby," while a few look as though they appreciated their business, by attending to it without making believe they know what their errand is. Everybody has a fancy of his own as to what is to be done, when, and how. But I must confess that I'm a "know-nothing."

A very important and humane arrangement has been instituted in this department, which deserves mention. The brave soldier who is killed, or dies by some frightful wound or lingering disease, is to be decently buried. The regiment or company to which a deceased soldier belonged are not to assume the responsibility of burial without an order to that effect from the Provost Marshal's office; each corpse is to be provided with a good substantial coffin, and if the deceased has no clean garments among his own effects (which must be proved), one is furnished, and a white board, with the name, rank, and age of the deceased neatly and legibly marked thereon. The relatives and friends of the deceased are to receive an official notice of the facts, detailing the manner of death, or sickness before death, and every item so far as known of the conduct of the deceased in the field. This is indeed an improvement on the old order of things.

The casualties have been large the past week, in comparison with what they have been in weeks previous; not less than 15 men killed since last Sabbath, and 21 seriously wounded. The rebels have been successful in spilling more loyal blood, but the day of retribution will surely come.

One of our hundred-pound batteries pretty effectually silenced the rebel work on the north end of James Island yesterday. I believe our battery has been ordered to keep open on them, while our men are at work on Gregg and Wagner. So long as our long guns pitch shell into the rebels, they have no chance of killing off the fatigue parties.

Monitor

[*Mercury*, November 3, 1863]

Morris Island, Oct. 24, 1863

Messrs. Editors:—We have no news of any great interest, save what would be considered contraband. Items are as scarce as birds' teeth; and everything and everybody is quiet as a burglar when the police are around. The rebels keep up a little gun practice daily, but the harm it does is very trifling, further than to make the fatigue parties do a little skedaddling behind the breastworks.

We heard pretty brisk firing on James Island last Wednesday, lasting about an hour and a half; but we have heard no particulars as to what it was. From the direction of the smoke of the guns, the firing must have been in the vicinity of the fight of July 16th.

It is rumored that a detachment of the 55th Mass. has been badly cut up; a detachment of 200 men are away from the regiment, but where they are no one knows; the fact of a number of the men being away, and the firing on James Island, may have given rise to the story; I cannot vouch for its correctness, and am inclined to think it is a canard.

The prospect of active operations is rather obscure; but of course those who know "what is what" don't mean that the secret shall be shared by the public or the "milishey" either. So all we have to do is grin and bear it. Morris Island begins to look as though civilized people were its inhabitants, but how can it be otherwise? Wherever the cosmopolitan Yankee goes, improvement goes with him; warehouses, docks and shipping are sure to spring up as soon as Mr. Yankee plants his feet, wherever there is land to put a house on and water enough to float a mud scow. His genius will make the land larger, or the water deeper, or else there is no virtue in machinery. Some of Johnny Bull's blockade runners may make a mistake before long, if Morris City progresses as it does now—they will take it that Uncle Sam's new city is Charleston, and run smack in before they find out their mistake. The navy remains quiet, with the indication of so continuing. But it is said that Admiral Dahlgren is seriously ill; the climate has acted very badly on his health, and it is very questionable if he ever completely recovers.[19]

The Monitors had a little "brush" last night. It seems the rebel ram undertook to come out, for what purpose is quite obvious; she got down the harbor as far as Fort Moultrie, when the little cheeseboxes opened on her savagely. The Monitors were walking round the harbor in fine

19. At one point Dahlgren wrote in his diary, "The worst of this place is that one only stops getting weaker. One does not get stronger. My debility increases so that today it is an exertion to sit in a chair. I do not see well. How strange—no pain, but so feeble. It seems like gliding away to death. How easy it seems!" Dahlgren apparently recovered for he remained in command until the end of the war (Dahlgren's diary quoted in ibid., 134).

style, evidently to get around the ram, to head her off, and capture her; but it is likely the rebels recollected the fate of the Fingal,[20] for the ram speedily made tracks for the city, well satisfied no doubt that the cheeseboxes are hard cases.

Shortly after the naval skirmish, there was a pretty brisk fire of musketry on Sullivan's Island; but it is probable it was nothing more than a picket encounter. The pickets are liable to fall in with each other nightly, in their aquatic perambulations.[21]

Old Sumter stands like a deserted castle, a lonely looking mark of departed power and glory. One can hardly realize when standing within less than half a mile of her crumbled walls, what a mighty sway she once wielded over this and the adjacent islands. She fires no gun now, neither do we see any men on the ruined walls. She must be practically deserted; only a few men left to preserve the name of possession. Her flag waves daily, but it is raised but a very few feet above the ruined walls and cannot be seen unless you are within a mile of the Fort, as it is rather unsafe for a man to show himself on the top of the wall. A Parrott gun is very quick in execution. The rebels have a continuous line of batteries from Moultrie up to Mount Pleasant, but it is shrewdly suspected that the most of them are "dummies." A few fifteen inch shell will soon reveal what they are.

Last Tuesday night there must have been an extensive conflagration in Charleston; the flames could be distinctly seen from Gregg for over three hours. While the fire was raging, the rebels ceased their regular gun practice, no doubt to view the scene going on at home.

Monitor

[*Mercury*, November 5, 1863]

Morris Island, Oct. 17, 1863

Messrs. Editors:—Since my last, little has occurred worth mentioning in affaires de guerre. But we may hope for something pretty soon,

---

20. Rebel ram *Atlanta*.

21. The rebel torpedo attack on *New Ironsides*, while not a complete success, came close enough to be perceived as a real threat to the Union fleet at Charleston. Thereafter, picket boats were put on guard every night, while two tugs circled protectively around the frigate (Hunter, *Year on a Monitor*, 144).

as there are indications that powder is soon to be used in very large quantities. To give the reasons on which I base my suppositions of early action would very likely get your humble servant in a rather complicated position, i.e., the Provost Guard House—but it is enough to say that the troops here have not been playing holiday at any time since Wagner was taken. And be it further known, that any department under command of a General like Gen. Gillmore will always earn the gratitude of the nation, —saying nothing about the government funds. If success be the fruit of perseverance, then the army of the South will be successful in an eminent degree, and every man feels sure of success; although none know precisely when, or how it is to be attained. They feel confidence in the head of affairs, and so long as men feel confident of their leaders, there is no such word as fail.

The rebels have been very quiet the past week. It is very unaccountable, but they let our working parties work almost the whole day without molesting them; but all the suspicious work is done under cover of night, so the rebels probably suppose the Yankees are only making themselves comfortable for the winter; but they may find out pretty soon that we want better accommodations than this sand patch affords; we want to know by experience whether the Mills House is equal to the Revere, or St. Nicholas, providing—it stands.

Last Monday, the obsequies of Ensign Howard took place. Ensign H. was wounded the night of the attack on the Ironsides; he lingered during the week, till Sunday last, on which day he died. He was said to be a very good officer, and his loss is felt to be a great one by both officers and men. He was followed to the grave by one company of marines, a squad of about 60 sailors, and a large number of officers from the fleet, headed by the Post band.

The health of the troops is improving since the cool weather has set in permanently; I have not noticed an ambulance pass by our street but twice during the past week, but I take the large number of men returning to duty as a test, rather than any diminution in the calls of ambulances.

Col. E N Hallowell returned to his command today. He is looking quite hale and hearty after his severe sickness, caused by wounds received before Fort Wagner on the 18th July. His familiar voice acted like electricity on the men on dress parade today, and Col. Littlefield says he never saw such an apt illustration of the adage that "sheep know the Shepherd's voice."

Died, Oct. 15th, of consumption, Nathaniel Jackson, of Hudson, N.Y., Co. A, 54th Mass. Vols.

Monitor

[*Mercury*, November 11, 1863]

Morris Island, Oct. 31, 1863

Messrs. Editors:—The past week has been one of active operations here with us. Last Monday at noon, the bombardment of Sumter recommenced with a vigor unparalled in the annals of warfare. By reference to my notes, jotted down as the events occurred, your readers will have a better understanding of the work going on than otherwise.

Monday noon, the three hundred pound Parrott was fired a little, to test her qualities; she commenced by putting one shot into Sumter. Then, feeling pretty well satisfied with that result, she half faced to the right and sent a shot whizzing into Moultrie; then, completely about face, she let old Fort Johnson have a taste of her sauce; still feeling a little more ambitious she right obliqued and sent a message to Castle Pinckney, which must have caused some commotion in the city, as Pinckney is not a great way from town. The rebels, thinking we were opening a regular engagement, assailed our batteries from all the positions. Moultrie, Bragg, Johnson, Simpkins, and one or two other batteries nameless to me, were soon blazing away at the Yankees for dear life, but I am happy to say they did no harm. After our side saw the rebels were "spiling" for a fight, they concluded to let them have a foretaste of what was to come on the morrow. Accordingly, the quondam rebel stronghold, Wagner, was let loose, and it was not long before the rebels were obliged to keep still.[22]

Tuesday morning, at 6 A.M., the battle began to rage. Wagner, Gregg, and the new battery midway between Wagner and Gregg opened all their powerful pieces on poor old Sumter. If Sumter was a wreck before,

22. Emilio says there were seven heavy rifles mounted at Fort Wagner (including a 300 pounder) and four in Gregg, plus two mortars that opened fire (*History of the Fifty-fourth*, 133).

how shall we express what she is now? Every shot fired at her hit, some of them going literally through the opposite wall. At 11 o'clock the monitors moved up in position, gave a few shots, and walked out, but the land forces never even relaxed their fire. Surely, but slowly, the great siege guns are doing their work; at each shot from the 300-pounder ton after ton of bricks, mortar and rubbish are toppled down into the water surrounding the grim old fortress. Moultrie and Johnson send a few shells over now and then, but they do but little damage. Boom! Boom! in pendulum regularity go the great guns, the sky in the north looks black, and the sun sets once more with the contending guns bellowing with vengeance; the mantle of night is dropped, but still the indefatigable Yankees are pounding the first refuge of armed treason. Two fresh monitors come up and relieve those that have worked since noon; strong, able men on shore are wending their way to the front to serve the guns all night; and long trains of wagons are going to Gregg, Wagner, and the new battery, loaded with shot, shell and powder. The way everything looks now is, that Sumter must and shall fall.

Wednesday, 28th.—The bombardment still goes on, but it is about the same as on the day preceding, a perpetual roar of artillery and a gradual opening of the east wall of Sumter. The outer wall is now a mass of debris, forming an inclined plane of about 25 degrees from the water to the top of the wall. The arches are plainly visible from Fort Wagner without the aid of a glass, but still the irrepressible 11th S.C. hold out, and indeed I see no reason why they should not. It is a question whether one shot out of a hundred thrown at the fort damages that particular corner that is inhabited. The rebels hold what may be termed the southwest corner, directly facing Fort Johnson, and in the position our batteries are, it can hardly be expected that we can damage that corner a great deal, as the projectiles would nine times out of ten glance off, thereby depleting our stock of ordnance stores to no advantage. So, in view of this, we have to be patient and wait to see how knocking down the east wall will affect the work.

Thursday, 29th.—This day, being one of a detail to report at Gregg, I had a good opportunity of seeing how things were progressing; from there could be seen the sad havoc made on the once formidable Sumter. The fort was at times enveloped in smoke for the space of 15 minutes, so rapid was the fall of shell, in and around it. At 10 o'clock, the flag and staff were shot off the wall and toppled in the water; then arose a shout from the gunners, pickets and fatigue party, with waving of hats, caps, and even shovels; every man left his work and mounted the parapets or anything that had an elevation of four or five feet, to see the thing. But, presto! amid the shouts and rejoicings, the bellowing of guns, the whizzing of ponderous balls, and the bursting of bombs over that doomed citadel, another flag is raised out of the black smoke, with the staff inclining greatly to one side; the balls are directed to it in rapid succession—the gallant rebel is forced to desist, till a lull, often occurring in a bombardment like this, enables him to appear again and set the staff firm and upright. After performing this daring feat, he coolly took off his hat, swung it around once, just in time to escape a 12 pound shot fired from a light field piece. After I saw this trick, you may be sure I had some grave doubts of ever getting the rascals out by this mode of attack, although they may be bombed out.

It is now Sunday, but still the battle goes on. The iron clads begin to show their abilities now; there seems to be especial inclination on the part of Moultrie to trouble them, for they lay right in range of her guns; but she has not given them a shot yet—they must make the dirt fly in Sumter, as all their shell are thrown inside. The old Ironsides will take the lead, I hear, when we get ready to talk to Moultrie.

I hope by next week's mail you will receive the gratifying news that Sumter is surrendered. But we have gone so far that we must go ahead. Thank the Lord there is no land left to build batteries on; we have got to Cumming's Point,[23] so if they want any shoveling done, they must begin on the next Island—Sullivan's.

Monitor

23. The northern tip of Morris Island.

6

Sumter Still Holds Out
Charleston, South Carolina, November 1863

The second heavy bombardment of Fort Sumter did not presage any new developments. Admiral Dahlgren had informed General Gillmore on October 20 that he would probably not attempt to remove the obstructions and enter the inner harbor until his expected reinforcements arrived. It was the beginning of a "drear and gloomy" season in which the high hopes of September and the frustrations of October would give way to resignation and even despair in the dark winter months ahead.

[*Mercury*, November 17, 1863]

Morris Island, Nov. 7, 1863

Messrs. Editors:—As I closed my letter last Sunday the guns were booming with a dull, heavy sound, and have been ever since, although not quite so many have been engaged during the past week as the one preceding. Sumter still holds out, and, to speak candidly, it is difficult to perceive any great change in the looks of the fort, after the lapse of a week. That part of the walls of the fort exposed to our guns is apparently battered down, as far as can be by artillery, be it ever so heavy and effective. From the top of the wall downward to within apparently 10 or 12 feet from the base, the material of which the wall was composed is entirely knocked down, some of the debris in and some outside the wall, so that the fort on that side (the sea front) presents the appearance of a regular sand work before it is sodded. Now, all the guns in

Christendom can never effectually displace the debris accumulated there, for the more projectiles thrown into the mass, the stronger it becomes. Not that Sumter is not practically and theoretically useless, for in reality it is, and very probably has been for some time. Day after day we shoot the flag away, the rebels content themselves with waiting till night, and then they put it up again; so, when daylight comes, we see it still floating proudly on the same old corner. Last Wednesday morning we saw a new flag raised on a longer staff, apparently both new; it floated about two hours, when it was shot away.

Last Tuesday, a deserter came over to Folly Island from James Island, and reported that on the day previous 11 men were killed in Fort Sumter and 27 wounded; he says that the rebels keep only a small garrison there in the day time, but reinforce nightly, to the extent of 400 men, removing them before daylight. We have been on the alert nightly, to hear of an assault being made on it, as it is "reliably" reported daily, that such and such a regiment is to "lead the charge on Sumter to-night"; but it has not come to pass yet.

"Fort Putnam" (Gregg) keeps up the fire now on Sumter, as "Fort Strong" (Wagner) is arranging her guns and embrasures for another point.[1] The other batteries are preparing for another vigorous campaign, and the "Reliables" say that Monday will inaugurate something stunning.

The rebels have kept pretty quiet, firing but very little. Fort Moultrie does not deign to give the monitors a shot, while they lay at anchor close to her, daily firing away at Sumter. Occasionally Moultrie throws a mortar shell over to Putnam or Wagner, but they do but very little damage. There must have been a little affair on James Island last Monday, as we heard pretty brisk firing and could see shell bursting high in the air, a little to the south of Seceshville.[2] We have heard

---

1. In honor of some of the Union officers who were killed during the operations against Charleston, captured sites were renamed, including Fort Wagner for Brig. Gen. George C. Strong, who commanded the first brigade in the July 18 assault against the fort, and Battery Gregg for Col. Haldimand S. Putnam, who commanded the second (Emilio, *History of the Fifty-fourth*, 134, 74, 88).

2. Before the war, Secessionville, on James Island, had been a hamlet of summer cottages. It was fortified by the Confederates and became the scene of a decisive Union defeat on June 16, 1862. Brig. Gen. Henry W. Benham, in temporary command at James

nothing in regard to it, as the most of the notables are quartered on Folly Island, and as a matter of course, the news is kept there.

As an item I will record the sailing of the Flag Vessel, cleared, from Lighthouse Inlet Tuesday, Nov. 3d, steamer Philadelphia, —to take her position among the fleet, off Charleston Bar.[3]

The sick and wounded of the 54th Massachusetts volunteers beg to acknowledge the receipt of a lot of hospital stores, kindly sent them by the benevolent citizens of New Bedford; and particularly to the committee, who interested themselves in carrying out the designs of the contributors. It is a gratifying proof that the poor soldier is not forgotten.

Monitor

[*Mercury*, November 26, 1863]

Morris Island, Nov. 14, 1863

Messrs. Editors:—Still the bombardment of Sumter progresses, and still the rebels are masters of it. The firing during the week has been principally carried on by mortars, keeping it up all night. From the long continued silence of our long Parrotts, it is very naturally supposed that we are preparing something in a new direction, to cooperate with the advance from this side. Everything looks auspicious and we may yet pounce upon Charleston before we are aware of it. Taking a place by storm or surprise is the work of a few minutes, provided you have assurance made doubly sure by preparing for it; and it is the preparation which takes time. However, we hope for the best. The rebels may be hard pushed for ammunition, as they fire but little of the improved patterns, compared to what they did in the early stages of the siege; or

---

Island, ignored orders left by General Hunter and mounted an attack in which Union troops were repulsed with great losses by a rebel force with barely one-third their strength. Confederate general Johnson Hagood claimed years later that this was a pivotal battle in the course of the war. Had Benham won, there was little to stop him from reaching Charleston (Davis, *Stand in the Day of Battle*, 56).

3. This was Admiral Dahlgren's flagship at Charleston. The flagship of the South Atlantic Blockading Squadron at its headquarters in Port Royal was the *Wabash*, an unarmored steam frigate (Hunter, *Year on a Monitor*, 103).

they may be witholding it for the iron fleet, should the Admiral's "bak bon" betray him into the temerity of running the gauntlet. The fire from the enemy is principally with the old fashioned mortar shell, 6 and 8 inch; no doubt some of the same stock stolen by that valorous Gen. Floyd.[4]

Although the booming of Yankee guns and mortars may keep the denizens of the city awake, it does not appear to impede home manufactures in the city, if we may judge by the curls of smoke apparently from factory chimneys.

The batteries on James Island, all below Simpkins, have remained silent for the last two weeks or more, which goes far to strengthen the impression that the guns are removed to some other point; probably to Sullivan's Island, just below the city, to command the channel. But those at and around Seceshville still remain, as we have both auricular and ocular proof almost daily.

The rebels have kept up a pretty brisk fire from Moultrie and Johnson the last two days; they seem determined to make our working parties uncomfortable as possible. Yesterday, the 13th, we lost five men killed in battery Chatfield, besides three wounded in Fort Putnam; among the killed was one man belonging to the 3d regiment, U.S. colored troops; two to the 11th Maine. I could not ascertain to what regiment the other two belonged.

But all the horrors of war are soon forgotten in the pomp and circumstance of show and parade. I observed this yesterday, probably more than I would at some other times. One of the brigades was out on the beach, trapped out in their best turnout for a grand review. The officers composing the staff were riding from one end of the column to the other, perfecting the line, disposing of guides, and giving all the usual and necessary orders. At the prescribed number of paces from the column, stood, sat, or lounged the usual crowd of lookers-on, soldiers from other brigades, who go to look at and criticise the evolutions. At this junc-

4. John B. Floyd, a former governor of Virginia and secretary of war under Buchanan, was among those whose corrupt activities were exposed by a House investigating committee in 1860. Floyd resigned, announced himself a secessionist, and returned home. One of his last acts was to order government ordnance transferred to arsenals in the South (McPherson, *Battle Cry*, 226).

ture, the stretchers are borne along from the front, dripping with blood, with the dead corpse of a companion in arms. The crowd gather round the stretchers—ask hurried questions, such as, what regiment does he belong to—what company, or, where was he hit? and a thousand such little questions, winding up with—poor fellow! it may be our turn tomorrow! which shows that, hardened as a soldier becomes, he feels solemn once in a while. While they look on in silence, the General who is to review the brigade appears—the band executes a grand flourish and plays a grand march as he rides down the line, which dispels every vestige of concern, or thought of the mangled corpses, hardly lost to the view of the lookers-on of a few moments before.

But it may be well that it is so. If a soldier gave way, and brooded over the chance and the probability of death, his life would be unbearable.

Monitor

[*Mercury*, December 4, 1863]

Morris Island, Nov. 21, 1863

Messrs. Editors:—Since the last record of events in this department, the bombardment of Sumter is still kept up night and day, and still the gallant rebels are masters of the situation—which, by the way, is a severe comment on the gallantry of Major Anderson in 1861.[5] But circumstances now may be the incentive to the rebels to hold Sumter, rather than any desire of historic fame, for it is positively asserted that the great bar to the iron clads' progress up the harbor is fastened to Sumter; and if we once get possession of Sumter, and let the chain drop to the bottom, which is stretched across the channel, then the monitors are to go in and demand the surrender of the city, as it is calculated that all the rebel batteries are not able to stop them. Such a belief is not unreasonable, if compared with what the iron clads have stood, in the way of shot.

This may account for the long delay in shelling the city from our present position—that Mr. Beauregard, who is a notorious chap for

5. Maj. Robert Anderson was in charge of the United States troops at Fort Sumter when the garrison was surrendered to the Confederacy on April 14, 1861.

taking exceptions, may have no shadow of complaint against us, of unfairness, or "violating the usages of civilized warfare," or acting in any manner objectionable to the ideas of Booli, Crapau & Co., in the siege of this "most refined city of America."

Last Monday night, the rebels opened a new mortar battery, in rear of the Moultrie house on Sullivan's Island, which occasioned some little excitement;[6] they no doubt expected to surprise us and completely shell us out, before we could possibly do anything to silence them; it was about half past ten, everything was very quiet, nothing but the regular shot or shell every ten minutes at Sumter breaking the quiet of the night, when the shell came through the air like so many firey tongued devils; seven mortars were opened in quick succession, keeping such a steady rain of fire on our batteries, pickets, and working parties, that they were forced to seek shelter. The telegraph flashed the news to headquarters that the enemy was endeavoring to shell us out preparatory to making a grand assault, —the whole force of the Island was immediately drawn out in battle array—the parrots and sea coast mortars were ordered to talk, and in thirty-five minutes the rebel invasion was a something out of the question. The next day, the monitors went up and gave them such a peppering that they have not fired a mortar from that battery since, and the Ironsides which the rebels had fondly believed was made useless by their nocturnal visit, let go from her mooring and took a trip up to Moultrie, gave them a salute of shot and shell, and then very coolly went back to her position and anchored, as much as to say "I still live Mr. Beauregard." In the engagement on Tuesday, one of the monitors got aground opposite Moultrie, and the rebels concentrated their fire upon her, but to no purpose—the extent of damage done was to riddle her smoke stack. She was aground for at least five hours, so that is a pretty sufficient proof of their invulnerability.[7]

Last night our forces made a reconnaissance around Sumter; one

---

6. Until then a hospital flag had flown over Moultrie House (Emilio, *History of the Fifty-fourth*, 138).

7. The monitor *Lehigh* ran aground on November 16. Despite a rain of shot and shell, a line from the *Nahant* was successfully carried to the *Lehigh*, and at the next high tide the vessel was pulled off the shoal (Hunter, *Year on a Monitor*, 162–63; Emilio, *History of the Fifty-fourth*, 138–39).

boat's crew more daring than some went up to the foot of the ruins and was hailed by the sentinel, the alarm was given and a lurid sheet of flame issued from Sumter, followed by the crack of at least four hundred muskets. Forts Johnson, Moultrie, Bee and Beauregard opened with grape and canister, and our party beat a hasty retreat. But where do the rebels keep such a strong garrison? The shot and shell falling in fort to all appearances leaves no room for 50 men, unless they have bomb proofs similar to what is in Wagner. But they *must* be got out, and I would suggest that we have a steam force engine, capable of squirting a column of liquid the distance from Gregg to Sumter; fill it with camphene, fluid, petroleum, or kerosene, or any other combustible fluid or oil, and saturate interior and exterior of the fort; the debris or anything else, becoming saturated with these combustible spirits or oils, would become ignited by the bursting of a few shell, and the heat from the flame would be so intense that the inhabitants of Sumter would be obliged to leave it. This may be considered rather ticklish, but, is it any worse than throwing red hot cannon balls, sticklers for humane proceedings? Get them out, any way. If they won't come out for one species of torment invent something hotter. War is nothing but barbarism at the best, and those who can excel in that, to put an end to a longer train of barbarisms, are in the end the most humane of the two.

Putnam and Strong are pounding at battery Simpkins on James Island to-day, making the mud and sand fly terribly; from the accuracy of our shots we gain the advantage of keeping them busy repairing damages. Johnson fires occasionally, but her fire does little damage. Moultrie fires none except a little daily practice, ricocheting shot, so as to sweep the water around the Northeast angle of Sumter in case of an assault.

What the intention of doing is, no one can divine; everything appears to go on as if we were to be established for life. The bombardment possesses no interest as it is going on night and day, and a lull in the booming of guns and mortars would be something extraordinary in itself.

Some of the men in the 54th have read with surprise that part of Governor Andrew's special message to the extra session of the General Court, recommending the Commonwealth to pay the troops of the 54th and 55th regiments the extra three dollars per month which the General government is too mean, or obstinate to pay. [We are] not surprised at the solicitude of the Governor to have us paid what we have so dearly earned, nor would we be surprised if the State would cheerfully assume the burden; but the Governor's recommendation clearly shows that the General Government don't <u>mean</u> to pay us, so long as there is a loophole to get out of it, and that is what surprises us, a government that won't recognize a difference between volunteers in good faith, and a class thrown upon it by the necessities of war. What if they do say that colored troops were raised in the Northern States merely by sufferance. A man who can go on the field counts, whether he be white or black, brown or grey; and if Massachusetts don't furnish the requisite number, why she must submit to a draft. But, we as soldiers, cannot call in question the policy of the government, but as men who have families to feed, and clothe, and keep warm, we must say, that the <u>ten</u> dollars by the greatest government in the world is an unjust distinction to men who have only a black skin to merit it. To put the matter on the ground that we are not soldiers would be simply absurd, in the face of the existing facts. A soldier's pay is $13 per month, and Congress has nothing to do but to acknowledge that we <u>are</u> such—it needs no further legislation. To say even, we were <u>not</u> soldiers and pay us $20 would be injustice, for it would rob a whole race of their title to manhood, and even make them feel, no matter how faithful, how brave they had been, that their mite towards founding liberty on a firm basis was spurned, and made mock of.

Monitor

[*Mercury,* December 15, 1863]

Morris Island, Nov. 28, 1863

Messrs. Editors:—The past week has developed nothing new in military affairs that we are aware of. The bombardment of Sumter seems to have been relaxed since last Wednesday, but what the object is in desisting is more than I can conjecture, unless it be that a further expenditure of ammunition is considered useless at present. But we do not expect that the lull will last long, as everything looks like a vigorous pushing ahead, and if something decided is not soon done it cannot possibly be for the want of either time, men or means. The troops here begin to feel a sort of impatient curiosity to see some fruition of their immense labor in making preparations. This has been one of the most arduous campaigns of the war, so far as steady endurance and sheer labor is concerned, and that too, under an almost tropical sun, and on an island totally void of antiscorbutic properties. The sentiment of the rank and file is "action."

The rebels are busy razeeing [razing] the Moultrie House to the ground; so it may be presumed they intend or hope to make our position a pretty warm one, ere many days shall have elapsed. Battery Simpkins and Pemberton take an opportunity now and then to annoy our men, in Putnam and Chatfield, but they generally get the worst of the bargain, as our Parrott guns are quicker in reaching them than their old 42's are in reaching us. The silence of Forts Johnson and Moultrie makes it plausible that the rebels are strengthening those forts to best advantage. The fire they have so recently passed through, in Wagner, Gregg and Sumter, has no doubt given them some valuable hints in defensive engineering, and it is important that our side batter them down before they become more impregnable than Wagner or Sumter.

It is reported that the steamer Planter, the same which was run out of Charleston harbor by Robert Smalls and turned over to the blockade fleet, has been captured by the rebels.[8] It appears that the vessel was bound round to Stono inlet, through Lighthouse inlet and the creek div[id]ing Cole and Folly Islands, but owing to the dense fog prevailing at the time, the pilot run her past the turn-off in the creek, continuing on too far up the inlet towards Seceshville. He did not discover his error until he ran in among the rebel picket boats patrolling the vicinity; when, as a natural [con]sequence she was captured. The pecuniary loss will not be very great, as the vessel was an old cotton dragger; but the fate of her crew may be a rather serious matter, for all except the captain and engineers are contrabands, and some of them formed a part of the crew who ran away with her. It is believed that Smalls was piloting her on the occasion.

8. Robert Smalls was a South Carolina slave employed on the rebel dispatch boat *Planter* when he commandeered the vessel in May 1862 and delivered it to the blockading fleet. Afterward he became a pilot in the U.S. Navy (McPherson, *Battle Cry*, 564).

Thursday last, being appointed as a day of Thanksgiving, the troops had a general holiday. The air was just cool and keen enough to make one feel that it was a genuine old New England Thanksgiving day, although it was not impregnated with the odor of pumpkin pies, plum puddings, and wine sauce, nor the savory roasts, boils and "schews" familiar to the Yankee homes of New England. But we made up the deficiency by the religious observance of the day in a very appropriate manner. It was a scene long to be remembered—a grand army assembled on the verge where old ocean roars, to render homage and thanks to the Great Giver of victory. The gilded star and waving plume of warring chief stood side by side with the humble citizen soldier or quondam slave! The famed cathedrals of the Old World never presented a scene more grand, majestic, and impressive than the volunteer soldiers of a great and powerful Republic, gathered in a solid mass, with the arching dome of heaven for their temple, acknowledging their dependence on the mighty King of kings. We had no rich toned and powerful organ to lull the warring passions into submissive reverence; but the waves on the sea-beat shore seemed to partake of the majesty of the hour, and in low and gentle ripples made music on the sands. Every head was bared as the Post Band commenced to play some of the good old Orthodox airs of home—no doubt reminding many there assembled, of the day as observed at home.

After the service was brought to a close, the respective regiments were dismissed, and the rest of the day was devoted to such sports as best suited each. The 54th had quite a good time considering the facilities at hand to create such a time. The officers of each company treated their men to what the Sutler's shops afforded, such as cakes, oranges, apples, raisins, besides baker's bread, and butter. Added to that, we had a greased pole set up, with a pair of new pantaloons tied to the end, with $13 in the pocket for the lucky one who could get it, by climbing to the top. The attempts made by some to win the prize were laughable indeed, and many who would not have been guilty of doing a hard day's work for the government, worked with a will on the greasy pole. One funny chap in Co. C, who is known by the title of Stonewall Jackson, was the first one to make an essay at climbing, which was not successful, except it be in taking one or two pounds of soap fat on his clothing to make an easy job of it for his followers. Poor old Stonewall said, "now I oughtenter took the first trial on that plagued pole, cause I've spoilt my clothes, and the Colonel will put me in the guard house, too, if my clothes aint clean on inspection." But the Quartermaster, enjoying the fun, and thinking Stonewall deserved something for his zeal, presented him with a new pair of pants for the pair he had spoiled. After the money was won by climbing the pole, we had a sack race. The purses were made up by officers, which were ten dollars for the first best, and five dollars for the second best; and in this contest poor "Stonewall" got entangled in his sack, so that he did not get three yards from the starting point. The next amusement was wheeling barrows, blindfolded, to a certain mark—the man coming nearest to the mark to receive five dollars, and the second to receive two dollars. So you see the boys are all alive and full of fun; they don't intend to be lonesome or discouraged whether Uncle Sam pays them or not; in fact the day was kept up by the 54th with more spirit than by any other regiment on the island.

To-day the conscripts and substitutes arrived by the steamer City of Bath, 84 hours from Boston.[9] The number is 73 men for the 54th and 160 for the 24th and 40th regiments. Among the subs is John Blackburn, of New Bedford, who is in Co. C. Company C has 11 men out of the 73 as her proportion.

Another marked feature in this department is an order recently issued, that all labor in the trenches and on batteries is stopped on the Sabbath day; that no duty is to be performed on Sunday, except what is imperatively necessary.

Monitor

9. The Conscription Act provided several options for a draftee unwilling or unable to serve. He could be exempted for physical or compassionate reasons, he could pay a commutation fee of $300, or he could hire a substitute (ibid., 601).

7

Waiting Till Something Turns Up

Charleston, South Carolina, December 1863
and January 1864

By the end of November it was apparent that any hope of occupying Charleston that year had long since been abandoned. Union artillery still fired on the city and its defenses, but the inner harbor now bristled with the additional guns that Beauregard had had time to assemble and that Admiral

Dahlgren was so reluctant to encounter.

General Gillmore, frustrated by naval inactivity and the resulting stalemate, requested permission in mid-December to send a portion of his forces in the Department of the South to occupy northern Florida.

[*Mercury*, December 28, 1863]

Morris Island, Dec. 12, 1863

Messrs. Editors:—The week just past has been one of unusual interest in the Department of the South. The first item is the loss of one of the iron monitors, on the afternoon of Sunday, Dec. 6th. The cause of her loss is enveloped in mystery to those on shore. We hear of a dozen different stories concerning it; some say that she was sunk by excessive rolling, as there was a heavy sea on at the time; while it is stated by others that she was sunk by a torpedo floating down the harbor; and others assert that some part of her boiler gear exploded and, forced downward, went through her bottom, thereby causing the catastrophe.[1] Putting aside all speculations as to how it happened, it will bring to the mind of many persons at home, as well as some abroad, that it was almost time that the "Iron Fleet" off Charleston had made itself famous for something more remarkable than "completing preparations." The country we think would feel better satisfied to pay a half million dollars apiece for every monitor before Charleston, providing they were sunk in a genuine endeavor to anchor in rebellion roads. If we don't look sharp, U.S. Grant may send fighting Joe Hooker to the rear of Charleston before the monitors have been cleared of barnacles![2]

The next item is the unfortunate penetration of one of our magazines by a rebel bomb shell. The shell came through a part of the magazine which the engineers were engaged in repairing, they having removed the sod and sand bags for the purpose of covering the top with four or five feet more of earth. The shell struck the top and broke through the roof, falling among a pile of capped shell, exploding twenty of them, besides a number of kegs of powder. The casualties resulting therefrom were four men killed, eleven men seriously wounded, and seventeen slightly, with the usual number scared—your correspondent among the last mentioned.

The next piece of news which you are no doubt apprised of through the Richmond papers, is the capture of Pocatiligo bridge by Brig. Gen. Seymour; so goes the yarn, on good authority too. The possession of this bridge by the Union forces may cut off some of the supplies of Charleston, but not to such an extent as to hasten a termination of the siege. It places Savannah in a rather tight position so far as direct communica-

---

1. The monitor *Weehawken* sank while at anchor with a loss of one-third of the crew (four officers and twenty men). A Court of Inquiry found that the weight of stores and ammunition recently loaded had put the vessel out of trim. Water coming in could not flow to the stern where the pumps were located, which caused the vessel to heel over to starboard and sink bow first (Hunter, *Year on a Monitor*, 169–70).

2. Ulysses Simpson Grant had recently been promoted to lieutenant general and put in charge of all the U.S. armies under President Lincoln. Brigadier General Hooker succeeded Ambrose Burnside as commander of the Army of the Potomac early in 1863 and quickly reorganized and revitalized the unit. His subsequent lack of military success against Lee at Chancellorsville led to his replacement by Gen. George Gordon Meade. Later, however, Hooker was recalled and he participated in the successful operations at Chattanooga in October and November 1863.

tion with Richmond is concerned; but still they have a circuitous railroad open through the interior of Georgia, unless Grant's army cuts them off at Atlanta. Still, holding Pocatiligo bridge is an advantage, which if backed by a sufficient number of men may induce the Commanding General to act independent of the "web feet," although going up to the rear may be a hard road to travel, as it must be expected the rebels have taken every precaution to hold the rear since the taking of Pocatiligo bridge.[3]

Gen. Gillmore seems determined to keep the citizens of Charleston awake, for hardly a night during the past week but what the rebellious city has been fired in some spot. Every night about 11 o'clock we open on the city. One night, being on grand guard at Fort Strong, everything was quiet as the grave, save the breaking of the droning swell on the beach, which made the quiet more intense. Hardly a breath of wind was stirring, when the roar of a 200-pound Parrott broke the silence. You could hear the missile whizzing through the air, and in just forty seconds, you see a sudden gleam—and hear a low rumbling noise, which plainly tells you that it has burst over Charleston. In five minutes the second shot is fired, with like effect, when you distinctly hear the alarm bells tolling, to warn the sleepy citizens of danger; and you observe James Island batteries signalizing to those on Sullivan's Island, when away they blaze with mortars and columbiads, vainly endeavoring to silence the "indefatigueables."[4] They have a mortar battery on Sullivan's Island, with seven mortars in it, which they let go every time we fire into the city, and you may suppose that there is a little noise about midnight, when the Yankees fire two pieces to the rebels' one.

Yesterday, Fort Sumter was in a blaze, but how it was brought about,

3. The story of the capture was only a yarn, as Gooding indicates in his letter of December 26. Pocatiligo lay south of Charleston on the rail line connecting that city with Savannah. Ironically, a year later the 54th was involved in actions around Pocatiligo for more than a month, and on Jan. 15, 1865, arriving at a bridge near the town, the regiment met up with Sherman's army driving from the West (Emilio, *History of the Fifty-fourth*, 266).

4. The columbiad was a long, heavy cannon used in coast defense. The ten-inch gun mounted on the sea face of Fort Wagner had made a number of damaging hits on the Union monitors assisting the first assault on Morris Island, July 10–12, 1863 (Hunter, *Year on a Monitor*, 101, 121).

I am at a loss to tell, unless the garrison set fire to the fort, or our forces have fired a few Greek shells into it. The fire and smoke were plainly visible from our camp all the forenoon, and till two o'clock in the afternoon.[5] While Sumter was in flames, the contending batteries were unusually active in pelting each other; fourteen mortars were steadily kept firing into Sumter, Fort Strong attended to James Island, Fort Putnam poured into Moultrie, and the 300-pounders shook the folks up in Charleston. I think every gun and mortar the contending armies have mounted were brought into play at that time, for the roar of ordnance was steady and terrible. It was not safe for a man to venture out of the entrenchments between Forts Strong and Putnam, so steady was the fall of fragments of exploding shell, or round and steel pointed shot. Col. E. N. Hallowell, while riding up to Fort Putnam, had his horse shot from under him but was not touched himself. The rain commencing about 2 o'clock yesterday afternoon, the firing ceased, and has not yet been renewed.

Monitor

[*Mercury*, January 6, 1864]

Morris Island, Dec. 19, 1863

Charleston Harbor Supposed To Be Clear Of Obstructions

Messrs. Editors:—Since my last letter, we have been on tiptoe, expecting to see or hear the iron fleet making an effort to get into Charleston harbor; but still the Philadelphia haunts the waters of Lighthouse Inlet, and the "invulnerables" preserve a masterly inactivity. For forty-eight hours, commencing on the 11th, a heavy easterly gale prevailed on the coast, causing a higher tide in and around the harbor than has been known since this army has occupied the Island, and on Sunday afternoon could be seen huge rafts and buoys floating about in the harbor and in the roadstead opposite the Island. After

---

5. Sumter's small-arms magazine exploded at 9:30 A.M., killing eleven men and wounding forty-one. There were rumors that a candle or sparks from a soldier's pipe may have set off the ammunition (Emilio, *History of the Fifty-fourth*, 141; Chaitin, *Coastal War*, 133–35).

some of these rafts and timbers had drifted ashore, it was apparent these formed the formidable obstructions in Charleston harbor; the timbers are, the most of them, six or seven feet in circumference and are covered with a coating of barnacles and shells, owing to being submerged so long. So far as the rafts indicate by their supposed position, the fleet could never have forced them sufficiently to pass without seriously damaging the motive power of the vessels, as it is very reasonably conjectured that the huge links of chain found attached to the rafts were cables to anchors or old guns, sunk to hold the raft in position directly across the channel, but short and heavy enough to keep the whole structure submerged, so that a hostile vessel could not be piloted clear of it. The rafts were apparently placed in sections, but each section was linked to the other by two bars of railway track, by means of car couplings bolted to the ends of each section. It may be that the naval authorities had a hand in loosening the grand network of obstructions in their nightly work upon them, fully expecting nature to assist them in the work, as it has done. But if they don't take advantage of what nature has accomplished for them pretty soon, the wily rebels will place a more complicated trap in their way. But they may be justified in supposing that the harbor is not clear; or, they probably know such to be the fact, but no one here has seen the navy endeavoring to ascertain whether the harbor was clear or not; they may prepare to reconnoitre by next spring.

How The Weehawken Was Sunk

I have just found out how the Weehawken was sunk. It is gravely asserted that the Admiral, in his afternoon siesta, saw the ghost of Sumter coming towards the fleet and telegraphed the Weehawken to run out of the way, and her speed, under the circumstances of fright and a bottom clear of barnacles, was so great that she ran under.

Shooting Of A Deserter

Thursday Afternoon, Dec. 18.—A special order made it the duty of all the troops on this island to witness a melancholy and impressive scene. —— Kimball, of Co. G., 3d N.H. regiment, a conscript recently brought out from Boston, deserted from his regiment and had got as far as our picket lines on the left. It is asserted that when he was discovered, he was signalizing to the enemy across the river to come with a boat and take him across; and after being taken, he represented himself as a rebel deserter, and the object of his signalizing was to direct a brother deserter, who had agreed to desert with him from the enemy. He was brought in to the guard on Black Island, to be sent over to the post headquarters in the morning, as no one doubted his story. He was disguised in citizen's dress at the time, and would have been paroled as a rebel deserter had not one of the men in his own company, who had been put into the provost guard house for some misdemeanor, recognized him. The delinquent soldier, seeing a rebel deserter, of course took a good look at him, just perhaps to see what a rebel looked like, when he suddenly exclaimed, "Hallo, Kimball, what the deuce are you doing here?" This familiarity excited curiosity, and when the guard saw the supposed deserter motion the soldier to keep mum, it created suspicion. An officer was called in and informed that something was wrong, whereupon there was an investigation, and the foregoing facts evolved. Several men from the same regiment were called and proved him to be a member of the regiment, whereupon he was court martialed, found guilty, and sentenced to suffer death. As before stated, on Thursday, at 4 p.m., the sentence of the Court was carried out to the bitter end.

The troops were formed in two columns of four ranks each, so the space occupied would be convenient for all the troops to witness the scene. Between the columns there was a space of eight paces for the funeral cortege to pass in review before the troops. An army hearse was driven through, containing the victim seated upon his coffin, preceded by a Martial Band playing a funeral march; the prisoner lounged upon his coffin, calm, and unmoved, except you might see a slight moisture of the eye; but his face was pale and careworn, like one who seemed to have hoped against fate, and now at the last was struggling to be resigned. He seemed to look each man in that vast assembly in the eye with a vague and melancholy appeal for sympathy, as the hearse drove down the line, which must have touched the hearts of many, although they knew he was guilty. After the cortege had arrived at the place of execution, he nimbly jumped from the hearse to the ground, and began to prepare himself for the final act in his drama of life. His head was shaved, and then the Chaplain offered a prayer; after that the Provost Marshall tied the fatal kerchief over his eyes, the officer of the guard put his men in position to fire, the Chaplain, Marshal and pall bearers shook hands with him, stepped aside suddenly; the officer shook his glove and the victim fell across his coffin; his feet trembled a moment and he was a corpse.

No sooner had the man fallen, a lifeless mass of earth, than a sea gull flitted over him, ready to pounce upon the first vestige of torn flesh that it might discover. This painful scene would have been totally devoid of incident, but for what the last mentioned occurrence gave to it. The appearance of the bird was so sudden, not one being in sight before, that it imparted to the scene a touch of the supernatural. It was only by repeated efforts that the guard was able to keep the voracious bird away. The lesson taught by the scene will no doubt be a lasting one to all who witnessed it.

Miscellaneous Items

The rebels opened pretty heavily on Tuesday last, but their fire did no extra damage. Last night about 11 o'clock, for the first time in a week, we opened on the city, which occasioned some savage firing on the part of the enemy, showing that firing on the city occasions more annoyance than they have admitted.

The members of the regiment represented by their noncommissioned officers are making efforts to celebrate the 1st of January in a becoming manner, the anniversary of the Emancipation Proclamation. An informal meeting was held last evening by the uncommish, and, of course, there was some rubbing of ideas. The only little incident that occurred worthy of notice was the wish expressed by some of the radicals to couch the language of the petition to the Commanding General for leave to make a celebration in such a manner as to convey the idea that the petition emanated from the soldiers of the department irrespective of class. The question was very warmly contested till tattoo, and it was unanimously agreed that the meeting was very harmonious!

Monitor

[*Mercury*, January 7, 1864]

Morris Island, Dec. 26, 1863

Strategy and Common Sense

Messrs. Editors:—Since my last there has been nothing extraordinary occurred in military affairs, and the indications are that nothing will occur between now and spring, unless brought on by the enemy. The whole face of nature now presents a drear and gloomy appearance, and the thousands who a month or two ago were full of hope and expectation have gradually come down to that frame of mind so well adapted to wait till something turns up. The fleet inside the bar has been steadily diminishing, so that there is nothing but the monitors and Ironsides left, together with three or four tugs, and provision/ schooners. The Philadelphia seems to have taken up winter quarters in the inlet, no doubt to save her from being rocked on the waves or the boisterous Atlantic. So, you see, Christmas has come and gone, but Charleston still holds her head high, as the leading city in the van of the rebellion. But then, Secretary Welles,[6] in his annual report, considers it to be no great matter whether the Union army occupies the city or not, as it is not, he says, any strategic point of value or commercial importance to the Confederate guerrillas. All that is very fine, as a defence of the miserable operation of the naval arm during the recent operations against that stronghold; but it will not possibly make the nation see why having it in our possession is not better than to leave it in the hands of the insurgents. Strategy or not, almost every one knows that the rebels depend upon Charleston for a very large amount of ammunition, which is manufactured there on account of its central position and being connected by all the interior lines of railway with different parts of the Confederacy. But the worthy old gentleman does not think that it would be any object to somewhat curtail these facilities, and it has not struck him as an idea, that in sealing Charleston up as a commercial help to the rebels, the most effective way is to take it, so that the fleet employed to watch it could be employed elsewhere. But the worthy Secretary is looking to the establishment of something stunning in war ships, which,

---

6. Gideon Welles, secretary of the navy.

as a precautionary measure, is very well. But do, good Mr. Secretary,
let us have the 4th of July in Charleston, and we will not regret not
having spent a merry Christmas therein so much.

Santa Claus in a Novel Shape

Yesterday (Christmas) morning, we gave the rebels in Charleston a Merry (or dismal) Christmas greeting, by throwing a few shell in
among them. The shell thrown evidently set fire to some part of the city,
as there was a grand illumination visible in a few minutes after the shell
were thrown. The wind being then from the northwest and the air very
clear, the sound of the church bells could be distinctly heard at Fort
Strong, but whether it was the regular ringing of Christmas bells by
the Catholic and established churches, or merely the alarm bells on
account of fire, is difficult to determine. From the hour (3 o'clock) it may
have been both circumstances that occasioned the loud ringing of bells
in the Palmetto City; one set of bells ringing to commemorate a glorious
event, bringing joy and mirth to the rising generation, and reflection
and thankfulness to those of mature age, —and the other, to warn the
guilty conspirators of the avenging flame thrown in their midst, ready
to leave them houseless, unless they make efforts to extinguish it.

Miscellaneous Items

Soon after, the rebel batteries on James and Sullivan's Islands
were opened, but with the same effect as heretofore—a waste of powder and shell; but about daylight we could hear very rapid and heavy
firing* on James Island in the neighborhood where our gunboats are
stationed in Stono river. I have not found out anything as yet in regard
to it, but I suspect the rebels were retaliating on the gunboats for our
firing on the city, and the gunboats of course must have given them as
good as they sent. I don't think it was anything more than for annoying
each other in that quarter; at least I shall wait till I hear something
more definite, as I may be sold a la Pocatiligo.

Christmas was rather a dull day with us, the 54th. But the 3d U.S.

had a stirring time—eating and drinking. Apple dumplings, equalling a young mortar shell in weight, with rye whiskey sauce, was the principal item on the bill of fare. So far as my observation went, apple dumplings formed the first and last course, but the boys enjoyed them notwithstanding the seeming lack of talent in the pastry cooks. The dinner to the boys shows a warm attachment between the shoulder straps and the rank and file, for the expense was borne by the officers.

The meeting referred to in my last, squelched by conservatives throwing cold water on the fire [fine?] spun plans of the radicals, adjourned sine die.

Hereafter Lieut. J. W. Grace ceases to be such—why? he will wear two bars on his shoulders, which it is hoped, will be replaced by two leaves—in time.

Monitor

*This was the attack on the Marblehead, the account of which we have published. [*Mercury* Editor][7]

[*Mercury*, January 14, 1864]

Morris Island, Jan. 2, 1864

Messrs. Editors:—All is quiet and evidently settled for the winter is the only conclusion to come to in regard to operations here. So, in absence of anything very exciting in the military line, I know of nothing that would be more interesting than a passing notice of the holiday observances. The first of January is of course the subject of great importance to the class whose service is the root of the peculiar institution. The day will henceforth be to the liberated slaves of the Southern States as dear and as hallowed as the "seventh year" was to the bondmen, spoken of in Holy Writ.[8] So yesterday, being "New Year's Day," the members of the 54th had the privilege of "spreading" themselves in "Solemn Convention." The observance commenced by the

7. General Beauregard's report of the incident is succinct: "Charleston, S.C. December 26, 1863—11.30 a. m. Expedition to destroy two gunboats in the Stono yesterday failed through bad firing of our batteries. We had 1 man killed and 5 wounded; 8 horses disabled. I will try another plan" (*ORA* 1, 28.1: 749).

8. "If your brother . . . is sold to you, he shall serve you six years and in the seventh year you shall let him go free from you" (Deut. 15: 12).

*w of New Bedford. Detail from the panorama of a "Whaling Voyage Round the ·ld" by Caleb Purrington and Benjamin Russell, ca. 1848. Courtesy, Old Dartmouth *torical Society.*

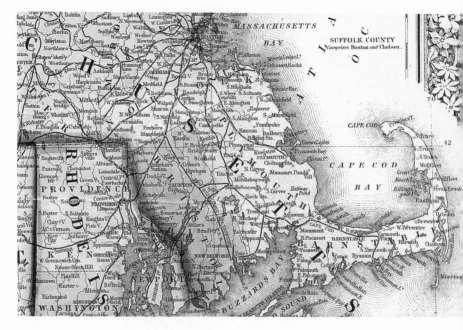

Southeastern Massachusetts. Detail from County Map of Massachusetts, Connecticut, and Rhode Island *(Philadelphia, 1862). Courtesy, American Antiquarian Society.*

COLORED MEN, ATTENTION!
YOUR COUNTRY CALLS!
One Hundred Colored Men Wanted.
To be attached to
Gov. Andrew's New Regiment,
THE MASSACHUSETTS FIFTY-FOURTH.

The Pay and Rations to be the same as those of any other Massachusetts Regiment.

The families of the Colored men enlisting to re ceive the same as that furnished white men in other Regiments

Head-Quarters for enlisting at the first building west of the Post Office, William street.

N. B —Colored men from any other town, city, or State. wishing to enlist, will be received the same as though they were from this city.

feb12   J. W. GRACE, Recruiting Officer,

Recruiting for the Massachusetts Fifty-fourth Regiment. Advertisement from The Mercury, *New Bedford, February 1863. In Norwood P. Hallowell Papers. Courtesy, Massachusetts Historical Society.*

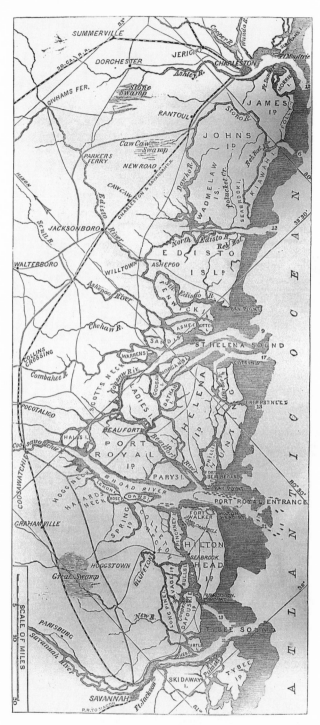

Map of the seacoast of South Carolina. From Harper's Weekly, *November 30, 1861. Courtesy, Old Dartmouth Historical Society.*

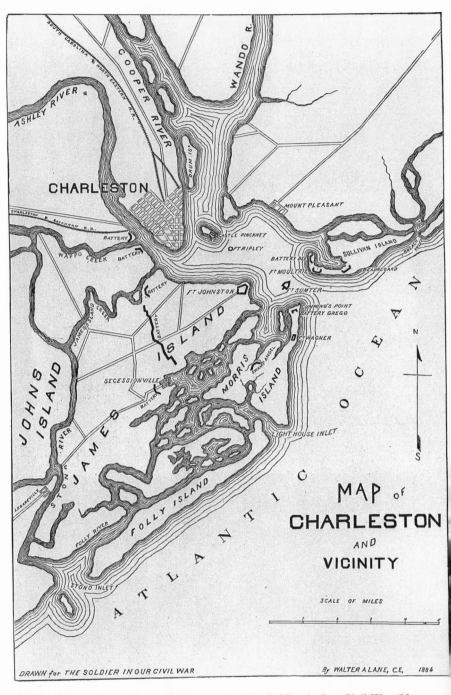

Map of Charleston and vicinity. Drawn for The Soldier in Our Civil War *(New York, 1884). Courtesy, Old Dartmouth Historical Society.*

Bird's-eye view of Charleston, South Carolina. From Harper's Weekly, *August 15, 1863. Courtesy, Old Dartmouth Historical Society.*

Storming Fort Wagner. *Chromolithograph by Kurz & Allison (Chicago, 1890). Courtesy, Boston Athenaeum.*

"The Appearance of the Ditch the Morning after the Assault on Fort Wagner." Pencil
drawing with gray wash and Chinese white by Frank Vizetelly, July 19, 1863. By
permission of the Houghton Library, Harvard University.

In the trenches before Wagner and (b) The mortar schooners and wooden gun-boats bombarding Fort Wagner and Battery Gregg. From Harper's Weekly, *September 5, 1863. Courtesy, Old Dartmouth Historical Society.*

The Seige *[sic]* of Charleston. *Lithograph by Currier & Ives (New York, 1863). Courtes*
Old Dartmouth Historical Society.

Interior of Fort Sumter after bombardment from Morris Island. From Harper's Weekly, *January 9, 1864. Courtesy, Old Dartmouth Historical Society.*

Ordnance depot, Morris Island, Charleston Harbor, South Carolina. From The Soldier in Our Civil War *(New York, 1884). Courtesy, Old Dartmouth Historical Society.*

Letter from the 54th (Colored) Regiment.

MORRIS ISLAND, Oct. 10, 1863.

MESSRS. EDITORS:—The monotony of life was somewhat broken last Monday night, October 5th, by an insane attempt by the rebels, to either capture or destroy the Ironsides. Their plans to destroy the vessel, were, to place torpedoes under her, and blow her up. The attacking party came down out of the inner harbor about 9 o'clock, passed the two monitors lying between Gregg and Moultrie, hugging themselves in the belief that they were unseen. But the ever watchful tars were very well aware of all the rebel manœuvres. They let them go ahead, as it was the intention of the navy to trap the bold rascals. After the rebels had made the distance opposite the Ironsides, by running close along the beach of Sullivan's Island, they struck boldly, but cautiously out for their prize. On they came, with muffled oars; but while they were approaching, the crew of the Ironsides were silently preparing to give their noctural or (infernal) visitors a warm reception. At length the rebel boats are within hailing distance—the marine on the bow of the Ironsides, cries—"boat ahoy!" no response from the boats, but sudden and vigorous strokes with the oars, and shouts of, "pull hard! the Yankees are all turned in—we've got her sure—pull, pull, lets get aboard before they awake." A rocket from the Ironsides told the monitors to begin—out of their huge guns, they threw grape, cannister and shrapnel—

(a) *Attempt to blow up the* Ironsides, *and (b) The "Segar Steamer." From* Harper's
Weekly, *October 31, 1863. Courtesy, Old Dartmouth Historical Society.*

Sinking of the monitor Weehawken, *December 6, 1863. From* The Soldier in Our Civil War *(New York, 1884). Courtesy, Old Dartmouth Historical Society.*

The city of Charleston fired by explosive shells from General Gillmore's guns in Fort Putnam, January 3, 1864. From The Soldier in Our Civil War *(New York, 1884). Courtesy, Old Dartmouth Historical Society.*

tle of Olustee, Fla. *Chromolithograph by Kurz & Allison (Chicago, 1894). Courtesy,* *ne S. K. Brown Military Collection at the John Hay Library, Brown University.*

(a) Massachusetts Memorial, Andersonville, Georgia, and (b)
Grave of Corporal J. H. Gooding, Andersonville, Georgia. Courtesy,
National Park Service, Andersonville National Historic Site.

Near Andersonville, *painting by Winslow Homer, 1866. Collection of The Newark Museum. Gift of Mrs. Hannah Corbin Carter, Horace K. Corbin, Jr., Robert S. Corbin, William D. Corbin, Mrs. Clementine Corbin Day in memory of their parents, Hannah Stockton and Horace Kellogg Corbin, 1966. Photograph © The Newark Museum.*

Camp of 54th Mass Colored Regt

1863.

Morris Island. Dept of the South; Sept 28th

Your Excellency Abraham Lincoln:

Your Excelency will pardon the presumtion of an humble individual like myself, in addressing you. but the earnest Solicitation of my Comrades in Arms besides. the genuine interest felt by myself in the matter is my excuse. for placing before the Executive head of the Nation our Common Grievance: On the 6th of the last Month, the Paymaster of the department, informed us, that if we would decide to recieve the sum of $10 (ten dollars) per month, he would come and pay us that sum. but, that, on the sitting of Congress, the Regt would, in his opinion, be allowed the other 3 (three.) He did not give us any guarantee that this would be, as he hoped certainly he had no authority for making any such guarantee. and we can not supose him acting in any way interested. Now the main question is. Are we Soldiers, or are we Labourers. We are fully armed, and equipped, have done all the various Duties, pertaining to a Soldiers life, have conducted ourselves, to the complete satisfaction of General Officers, who. were if any, prejudiced against us, but who now accord us all the encouragement and honour due us: have shared the perils, and Labour, of Reducing the first stronghold, that flaunted a Traitor Flag: and more, Mr President. Today, the Anglo Saxon Mother, Wife. or Sister. are not alone, in tears for

Letter to Abraham Lincoln from James Henry Gooding, Morris Island, September 28, 1863. Courtesy, United States National Archives.

Bark Sunbeam *of New Bedford. Courtesy, Old Dartmouth Historical Society.*

(a) Record of Seamen's Protection Paper issued to Henry Gooding, New Bedford Custom House Records. (b) Henry Gooding's account in voyage accounts of Bark Sunbeam, *1856–1871, J. & W. R. Wing Collection. Courtesy, New Bedford Free Public Library.*

THE SAILOR'S REGRET.

COMPOSED AT SEA,

BY HENRY GOODING.

Oh, bury me not 'neath the wide rolling billow,
Where the wild seabird will cry over me,
But let me lay 'neath the old weeping willow,
Far, far away from the tempestous sea.

Oh, let me lay near my departed sires,
In the old churchyard, where wild flowers grow,
So that at eve, when the sun it retires,
Friends, they may gaze where I am laid so low.

Oh, bury me not where the wild ocean's foaming,
Where hollow winds unceasing do roar ;
But take, Oh, take me when I am done roaming,
And lay me down on my own native shore.

For there dwells my loved one, Oh ! there dwells my
      mother,
There dwells all on earth that to me is dear ;
There is my father, my sister and brother,
Within their dear gaze Oh, do lay me near.

Well do I know that many a wild rover,
Has craved a grave 'neath the wide rolling deep,
But as for me, when this weary life is over,
In my own native land I want to sleep.

"The Sailor's Regret" by Henry Gooding. Courtesy, Old Dartmouth Historical Society.

IN MEMORY OF
ELI DODGE,
WHO WAS KILLED BY A WHALE,
Sept. 4, 1858, off the Coast of New Holland.

COMPOSED AT SEA,

BY HENRY GOODING.

He has gone from our gaze, he'll never more return,
A shipmate we all did revere,
We no more of him, our duty will learn,
No more with us, will he make cheer.

He had perhaps a dear cottage home,
Or maybe a sister or a brother,
Who knows but a wife,
The joy of his life,
A child, or a fond loving mother.

He was brave in the storm,
He was kind in the calm,
His duty he done like a man,
But now he is free from this world's alarms,
And safe moor'd in the Spirit land.

He ofttimes with us did the monster pursue,
The huge monster king of the deep,
But now he is gone, and his journey is through,
Where loud billow's roll he does sleep.

How little we thought, but a moment before,
When near us he bravely did contend,
With the huge monster then weltering in its gore.
That he would to hades Eli send.

But he's gone from our gaze, his long race is run,
In death's cold embrace he does lie,
Yet Father of Mercies Thy will be done,
And take his soul to Thee on High.

"In Memory of Eli Dodge" by Henry Gooding. Courtesy, Old Dartmouth Historical Society.

Memorial to the Fifty-fourth Regiment of Massachusetts Volunteer Infantry (Colored) *by Augustus Saint-Gaudens, Boston Common, dedicated 1897. Courtesy, Richard Benson and Eakins Press Foundation.*

marching of a guard of honor to the parade ground. The object of this guard was to keep outsiders at a respectful distance from the raised dais, prepared for the orators. Sixty men composed the guard, fully armed and equipped, under the command of an Orderly Sergeant, who was "officer of the day" and general supervisor of the militia, having two second Sergeants as "aids." The balance of the men were, for the nonce, supposed to be citizen, and each company was designated by some popular civic title; each society as it came to the square to the right of the Colonel's quarters had its position assigned by the committee of arrangements. The civic possession [procession], preceded by the regimental band and drum corps, marched down to the 2nd South Carolina and 3d U.S. camps, taking a large deputation from each to represent those two regiments, and then marched to the square mentioned above; the militia presenting arms, as the civilians were coming to the position assigned.

The Exercises

Were inaugurated by prayer from the Chaplain, after which the Musical and Vocal Club executed and sung the "Year of Jubilee." The presiding officer of the day (civic) then announced Sergeant W. H. W. Gray, as speaker.[9]

The sergeant thanked the committee for their consideration in conferring such distinguished honor upon himself and said—"Fellow Soldiers, I am proud to meet you here on an occasion like the present, and I believe that you all feel the significant teachings of the hour. It is something to say, it is something to deck the page of history, that on South Carolina soil the race that her laws have been studiously framed to oppress, on the 1st of Jan., 1864, stand upright as living men, with irresistible arguments in their hands, to make their liberty permanent. Yes, we have cause to rejoice today, for the steps we have taken can never be retraced, the mite we have gained can never be snatched from our tenacious grasp, if we but watch the course of events, and remain

9. First Sgt. William H. W. Gray was a thirty-eight-year-old seaman from New Bedford. A member of Company C, he had been wounded in the assault on Fort Wagner. In September 1863, he organized a Masonic lodge on Morris Island (Emilio, *History of the Fifty-fourth*, 129).

faithful and true to ourselves, to our God and our country." The sergeant's remarks would have been very appropriate had he not taken occasion to revert to the pay of the regiment in a manner a little bombastic. The next speaker was Sergeant Barquet.[10] The remarks of Sergeant Barquet were very instructive. After congratulating his comrades on the privilege of enjoying such a day on the soil of the "nullifiers,"[11] he made a comparison between the real friends of liberty of today and those of a few short years since, showing that the men who had been looked upon as models of fidelity and patriotism only a few years previous to the war were now the bitterest opposers of freedom to the masses and republican institutions. He said he did not wish to be understood as meaning that a man should belong to any party in particular to make him worthy of confidence, for some who had been on the abolition platform were only on it for political power, or to gain some advantage over their fellows. In fact, he seemed to have a very keen perception of the machinations of parties, so far as the black man is their subject. He wound up by comparing the sentiments expressed by the Hon. J.M. Mason, six years ago at the foot of Bunker Hill, at the inauguration of a monument to the brave Gen. Warren, with his conduct since that period, one of the moving spirits of the unholy rebellion, and not only a sympathizer with, but an active and politic agent in Europe for a power to be raised on the ruined liberties of the humble masses.[12]

10. Joseph H. Barquet was a forty-year-old mason from Galesburg, Illinois, who served to the end of the war in Company H. Emilio reports that on this occasion the box serving as speakers' platform collapsed, carrying him down, but Barquet, not the least disconcerted, shouted from the wreckage: "Gentlemen, I admire your principles but damn your platform!" (ibid., 144).

11. South Carolina was the most notable upholder of the principle that states had the right to decide on the constitutionality of federal laws. On the issue of the tariffs of 1828 and 1832, South Carolina passed an Ordinance of Nullification declaring the tariffs unconstitutional and therefore null and void.

12. James Murray Mason was United States senator from Virginia from 1847 until March 1861, when he resigned to join the Confederacy, and he represented the South in London until the end of the war. The hero of Bunker Hill was Joseph Warren, a Boston physician, member of the Boston Committee of Safety, drafter of the Suffolk Resolves (1774) advocating forcible resistance to the British, and despatcher of Paul Revere on his famous ride to warn of the British march on Concord. Warren was killed during the Battle of Bunker Hill, June 17, 1775.

He quoted the following sentiments from Mr. Mason's speech of that day, which are worthy of perusal now, "If that great and gallant man (Warren) could have returned from the battle field and told Massachusetts to hand down the memory of that day from generation to generation, posterity would have found his request fulfilled. Four generations have passed by; we are here in the fifth now. I shall tell it in old Virginia, when I return to her hallowed land, that I found the spirit of Massachusetts as buoyant, as patriotic, as completely filled with the emotions that should govern patriotism, when I visited Bunker Hill, as it was when that battle was fought."

The Sergeant's conclusion was that the Senator is a fair specimen of men who preach a doctrine, but never suppose they will be expected to follow what they preach; although he gave Mr. Mason the credit of being converted to the monster secession by the pressure of circumstances. Corporal Jones[13] was the next one to address the assemblage, and his remarks were very appropriate, notwithstanding his evident partiality to Webster's great masterpiece. The substance of his remarks was, that the fact of the colored man being a part and parcel of the military arm of the nation was a sufficient guarantee that he was not a brute, but a man; and as a man, the future was full of hope for him; for the nation is contending for the rights and liberty of not one class or condition of people, but the struggle now going on is for all, that the institutions framed by the revolutionary patriots may be a reality, and not a name. He urged his comrades in arms to remain hopeful, and not cease in their efforts to gain, if possible, a more lasting name than what has been accorded them for that bloody night before Fort Wagner. He said that night's work would be a bright example, but warned them not to vainly suppose that would be a sufficient sacrifice for liberty and freedom of the race. In conclusion, he said—no matter how much the enemies of liberty seek to deride our efforts and treat us with contempt, they dared not insult or molest him, while he had the United States uniform on, and a consciousness of right on his side. The next person announced was Sergeant Jones of the 2d S.C. regiment. His remarks were not lengthy, but he was very earnest; he told the boys he was

13. Cpl. Alexander Jones of Company D was from Pittsburgh. He died of disease the following July at Beaufort, South Carolina.

happy to meet them on an occasion like this, and all he could say was "to fight hard, and never flinch when they meet their enemies." Sergeant Welsh[14] was called upon to say a few words, and he very happily put the audience in a roar, by saying—"as you have called upon me to speak, and will insist, don't blame me if it is a very poor one, so all I can say is—if we meet the rebs, why tuck it to 'em." Sergeant Fisher[15] was the next one announced, but as he was very much like a ship at sea, without a compass, the world will remain in blissful ignorance of his sentiments. After Sergeant Fisher's homily, the Chaplain ascended the forum and gave a very interesting exposition of the Constitution as regards slavery. He contended that it was not a Constitutional Institution, inasmuch as the Constitution could not be used to abrogate it in any state, and per contra could not be used to sustain; that slavery, so to speak, existed merely by sufferance in direct opposition to the moral principle of the people both North and South, and it was only by the corruption of parties that the leaders of the rebellion were lured into the vain project of founding a new empire, with the slave population to be a sort of peasantry, as it was under the aristocracies and despotisms of the Old World. But he thanked God that the loyal people were alive to these truths, and would, rather than see their country destroyed,—call in the aid of every man to uphold the heritage of Liberty, let his hue be what it may. In conclusion, he showed how the anniversary they were then celebrating was but a sure sign that the designs of traitors were defeated.

After the Chaplain had concluded, all hands joined in the John Brown song,[16] after which three times three were proposed to the memory of Col. Shaw. It is hardly necessary to add that it was responded to with a will, each man uncovering, accompanied with the flourish of bugles, the rolling of drums, and drooping of colors.

The exercises were announced to be concluded, and the men were

14. First Sgt. Frank M. Welch, of Company F, was a twenty-one-year-old barber from Meriden, Connecticut. At his discharge in August 1865, Welch held the rank of first lieutenant.

15. Albanus S. Fisher, aged thirty-two, was from Norristown, Pennsylvania.

16. One of the most popular marching songs of the Civil War, with its chorus of "Glory, Glory, Hallelujah," the John Brown song used the melody of an old Methodist camp-meeting hymn for which Julia Ward Howe wrote new words. These were published in February 1862 as "Battle Hymn of the Republic" and were an instant success.

marched off, eminently satisfied with the manner the day had been spent.

Monitor

[*Mercury*, January 21, 1864]

Morris Island, Jan. 9, 1864

Messrs. Editors:—The Union army before Charleston may be justly compared to that of the allied forces in Flanders, in the time of William and Mary. It is here without any definite prospect of accomplishing its mission, at least from the position now held in the front. It is not very surprising that the public are no more interested in the siege of Charleston; that they regard with suspicion the sensation[al] despatches to the press, calling on them to keep their ears open for the stirring news which is sure to be brought by the very next steamer. The game is about played out, and none are so dull as not to see that but very little has been done towards the reduction of Charleston. Had half the alacrity and vigor been exhibited in the prosecution of the siege of Charleston as was displayed by Luxembourg before Mons,[17] the undertaking, if not successful, would have a fairer record than it will in the eye of an impartial historian. If it is claimed that the two positions bear no resemblance, it can with equal justice be urged that the means of attack are immeasurably in favor of the tactician of today. In the wars that distracted Europe in the 16th and 17th centuries, a 20 pound shot was as wonderful as a 200 pounder is now. If the reduction needed the service of part of the forces at another point there is one almost the counterpart of Aghrim. Jinkell was bent on obtaining possession of Limerick; his coadjutors did not deem it a sure thing; but his intrepid reasoning surmounted all difficulties, and through a glorious battle of two hours his victorious army entered the fort.[18] The same could be

17. Francois Henri de Montmorency-Bouteville, duc de Luxembourg, commanded French troops in Flanders during the War of the Grand Alliance, 1688–1697. Mons, capital of Hainaut province (now part of Belgium), was a fortified town often fought over in the seventeenth and eighteenth centuries.

18. Gen. Godert de Ginkel, in command of William III's troops in Ireland, won a

done here, and we should soon have the rebellious city at our mercy, by a very few miles marching to the north of James Island. But it is more than probable that the wily rebels have fortified themselves strongly from where they slaughtered our men in 1862,[19] all the way to the northern extremity of the Island, determined to make a steady and dogged resistance. If they are wise, they must have their position made comparatively secure against surprise, and as a consequence the reduction of Charleston will be as if newly begun. It is idle to suppose that the rebels will relax their exertions to make the entrance to the harbor more intricate than it was during the last summer, if intricate it was; for recent developments show that by a little perseverance the formidable obstructions could have been removed, or so dexterously evaded as to have admitted the iron fleet into rebellion roads.

It is folly to suppose the rebels, reduced by reverses in the field, financial embarrassments, and the apathy exhibited by the great powers of Europe, will be so foolish as to give up their scheme of independence; simply by resisting and holding their position, if need be for a number of years, so that the powers of Europe will, by the simple fact of their ability to resist a mighty power, recognize them as a member of the family of nations. It is this last and forlorn hope that keeps the fire in the hearts of the leaders, and they will fight so long as there is an organized body to handle; and Charleston will be defended if every other city in the Confederacy must fall first; for like the Highland Chief, Glencoe, Charleston will stipulate for the proud honor of submitting the last to force of the Union arms, as the barbarous chief did, too late, to the British Power.[20]

But the chief duty of the hour is to keep ever before the insurgents

---

decisive victory for the English on July 12, 1691, at Aughrim (or Aghrim), a small village in County Galway. The Irish were strongly positioned behind marshy ground but Ginkel was able to penetrate their defense. His success led to the surrender of Limerick and ensured the reconquest of Ireland.

19. Secessionville.

20. Required by the British to take an oath of allegiance by Dec. 31, 1691, proud Alexander MacDonald of Glencoe delayed until the last moment. Then an unlucky circumstance made him late and gave the English government an excuse for punishment. The treacherous Campbells provided the means, and a bloody massacre of MacDonalds ensued.

not only the semblance of the National Power, in numbers of men, guns and ships of mail, to intimidate them, but we must make them feel the power we wield, and see then if the Southern press will treat our efforts with derision. If the war should end tomorrow, without Charleston being subjected, our victory would be great, to be sure, but the insurgents would exultingly boast that the first city that sullied the national honor could never be subdued. For the sake of the national honor let Charleston be taken before the war is over.

Monitor

[*Mercury*, January 28, 1864]

Morris Island, Jan. 17, 1864

Messrs. Editors:—Since my last nothing has transpired of importance. The shelling of the city is carried on with almost ceaseless persistency, at intervals of 15 minutes, day and night. The rebels do not seem to reply so readily as heretofore from their batteries on James and Sullivan Islands; but it may be it is because they are short of ammunition and think it prudent to husband it for an emergency. There is a yarn "going the rounds" that one of those "persecuted loyalists," who recently escaped from Charleston, brings intelligence of two monster guns planted on the marine parade in that city to dispute the passage of the Ironsides. It is gravely asserted that the guns mentioned will throw a projectile weighing 700 pounds! I wonder if there is not a similarity between these "rebel deserters" and the "bidders" at the "Peter Funk" sales.[21] It seems very strange that men can desert from the rebels so easily and can't from us; may be Mr. Beauregard sends the rascals over here to scare us with tales of guns and men, so as to keep us from coming too close to him. They are bad enough to do worse than that, and may be foolish enough to think it will do good.

On Friday the 15th about noon, very heavy and rapid firing was heard, which, from the direction of the sound, was in the Stono river well up to the rear of James Island. Taken in a direct line from Fort

21. Auctions at which spurious bids are made or announced in order to stimulate bidding and raise prices.

Johnson in a westerly direction, it could not have been over three and a half miles from the city. If it was from our gunboats, they were up further than their firing has indicated before, although it may have been a salute fired by the rebels from some of their interior batteries on the Island. What they can have achieved to justify them in wasting powder is a puzzle, unless it be in honor of Mr. Meminger's new financial scheme, or Mr. Mallory's "most successful undertaking during the war,"—that one, that didn't go![22]

Capt. James W. Grace has been transferred from Co. C to Co. A, but it is against his desire to be parted from a company he has been so long identified with. But duty made it necessary for him to change, and like a true soldier he knows no alternative, and he obeys. It is hardly worthwhile to say that the company is sorry he is not to be their commander, although it is still hoped he will be returned to his old command.

Glancing over the advertisements in a daily, my eye caught the following:

"Young men having a fair common-school education and physically sound, and especially privates and noncommissioned officers in the army, who desire to command colored troops, are invited to become students of this school."[23]

A school to prepare young men to command colored troops! Not to be ironical, some of the young men who can consistently go to this school may want a few hints as to the best mode to command themselves. It may be the Supervisory Committee never dreamed that there might be some colored young men who, by virtue of enlisting and serving in the ranks till promoted through the different grades to Orderly Sergeants, were just as capable of being entrusted with the command of colored

22. Christopher Memminger was secretary of the Confederate treasury; Stephen R. Mallory was secretary of the Confederate navy.

23. The Free Military School for Applicants for Command of Colored Troops was the brainchild of Philadelphian Thomas Webster and began operating there in late December 1863. It was a "cram school" for candidates who needed help in passing the examination required for officers commanding colored troops. At that time about 50 percent of those taking the exam were failing. In its first ninety days the school's success rate was 96 percent. The school closed Sept. 15, 1864 (Joseph T. Glatthaar, *Forged in Battle: The Civil War Alliance of Black Soldiers and White Officers* [New York, 1990], 45–47).

troops as those who know nothing of the dispositions or feelings of such troops. Perhaps the copperheads will say, "Why, bless me, are the Negroes beginning to show a penchant for promotions already!" Well, why should they not? Is it a crime for a man to aspire to something higher, providing he is capable and has a claim to do so? Can the nation expect to see the black man show the same ardor and enthusiasm fighting the battles of the Republic, when their claim to justice and fair play is persistently ignored or purposely lost sight of?

To be sure the great boon of liberty and enfranchisement is something, but it need not be ostentatiously paraded as a sufficient equivalent for the service the black has or may render. Presuming it to be the policy of the government to keep the black man as a part, even, of the military arm of the nation, could it reasonably be expected that one could be induced to enlist, when he knew that his chances of remaining a subaltern were greater than to become anything higher. Supposing we became involved in war with some foreign power, the incentive to the black man to fight would not be the same as in this war. Nothing but the mere fact of his being then a soldier, and performing a duty from the principle that he merely fulfills a contract, would prove of avail to incite him to deeds of valor. He would not even have the poor satisfaction of knowing his service was appreciated; for appreciation, by the law of comity, has the element of reward for the service. It is all very well to pat a battle-scarred soldier on the back, and say "you're a brick, old chap"; but people stroke a dog, or play with a monkey on the same principle! Some naturalists have labored very hard to prove that a black man is not human, hence the caution in trusting him with even limited responsibilities. We will not mention Charles O'Connor's position; it may be familiar to many, although it does not relate to the negro in a military point of view, for he did not foresee the probabilities of the negro becoming a part of the military arm.[24] But the gentlemen who first inaugurated the school referred to are somewhat colored with his ideas in one respect at least. Mr. O'Connor says "they (the negroes) are of no use, unless they have the master mind of the Caucasian race to

24. Charles O'Conor was a well-known New York lawyer who supported slavery and the right of the South to secede.

direct or coerce them." It is a fair presumption that the committee have the same ideas regarding their military capacity.

Monitor

[*Mercury*, February 5, 1864]

Morris Island, Jan. 23, 1864

Messrs. Editors:—War matters are enveloped in mystery here and everybody is now conjecturing "what is to turn up." The gentlemen of the press are gone, no one knows where, but it is very likely they are where news is expected of a stirring character. Gillmore's express trains leave Putnam and Chatfield stations every fifteen minutes for Charleston,—through without stopping—time, thirty to forty seconds. The rebels were in the habit of firing on our transport steamers in their passages from Stono Inlet to this post, but since opening a battery from the upper end of Folly Island, in Seceshville, the rebels have no doubt come to the wise conclusion that to let us alone is the best policy.

We are enjoying delightful weather at present and have been for the last week; it is equal to a northern May, minus the rains. What a country this will be to live in, when the Star of Peace reigns once more supreme, and that bane of its life, slavery, will only be known in history! when the poor and ignorant can feel that their home is not a land of oppression; and the rich and affluent can rest secure, without the ever constant dread of servile insurrection, massacre and pillage! When we reflect, and take into consideration the characters and pursuits of the men who inaugurated the present rebellion, we cannot but be assured that they love anarchy and ruin in preference to liberty and peace. Had they been let alone as they desired, they would not have sought to better the condition of their country or its people, neither would they be content to let us pursue a system of popular government unmolested; for the power and strength they possessed when they undermined the government, if suffered to go their way, would in a few years be augmented to such an extent that the peaceful homes of New England men would not be safe from invasion by a usurping slave power. So in this view of the case, it is encouraging to think that the most beautiful portion of this continent will be eventually the birthplace of a free and industrious people.

An accident occurred on Thursday morning in this wise; three of the guard of the 2d South Carolina regiment were seated on boxes close together, eating their breakfast, when a man belonging to the regiment, just come in off picket guard, was going past to a place near the guard tent assigned for discharging the pieces of those coming off guard. Unfortunately, the man with the loaded piece, as he came near where the three men were sitting, his gun resting on his arm in a horizontal position, let the hammer fall, and the ball passed through the jacket of one of the men, grazing the flesh slightly, and through the shoulder of the other, and lodged in the head of the third one, killing him almost instantly.

We have had an arrival of recruits, among the number are Joseph Wilson and Charles Washington, of New Bedford.[25] The regiment begins to merit its title to good discipline and military bearing, for which it was so famous before the campaign in the trenches before Charleston.

As there is no news, I shall bring my letter to an end, hoping that ere another week shall pass, there will "something turn up" worthy of being recorded.

Monitor

25. Joseph T. Wilson, like Gooding, had been a whaleman before the war and was wounded at the battle of Olustee. Wilson survived, however, and after the war was the first black member of the Grand Army of the Republic, becoming a colonel and aide-de-camp to its commander-in-chief. In 1882 he was asked to write a history of black soldiers in the United States, which was published six years later as *The Black Phalanx: A History of the Negro Soldiers of the United States in the Wars of 1775–1812, 1861–'65* (Hartford, Conn., 1888).

8

I Am Pained to Inform You
South Carolina and Florida, February 1864

On January 13, 1864, President Lincoln wrote to General Gillmore directing him to proceed with plans "to reconstruct a loyal State government in Florida."[1] The expedition was to be led by General Truman Seymour, who had also commanded the July 18 assault against Fort Wagner. Seymour took with him a force of about 7,000 men that included the Fifty-fourth Regiment. They arrived at Jacksonville on February 7 and the next day, leaving a disappointed Fifty-fourth behind for picket and guard duty, the other troops began moving west along the rail line, engaging in skirmishes with the enemy as they went. Later the Fifty-fourth was relieved by the Massachusetts Fifty-fifth Regiment and joined the troops advancing on Olustee.

General Seymour was acting in defiance of orders from General Gillmore as he moved toward the rebel line. He was evidently also completely ignorant of the extent of the enemy's strength. In the early afternoon of February 20 the opposing forces met. Wave after wave of Union troops was driven back by murderous fire from the Confederates. In mid-afternoon Seymour realized that the battle was lost and sent for the colored brigade to cover his retreat. The Fifty-fourth Regiment had been resting some distance from the fighting awaiting orders. Throwing aside knapsacks, blankets, and haversacks, the men marched at the double-quick, arriving at the battlefront at about four o'clock. They were placed on the left flank and remained there while all the

1. George F. Baltzell, "Battle of Olustee," *Florida Historical Quarterly* 9, no. 4 (1931): 201.

other regiments retired. *The Fifty-fourth stood alone holding back the enemy. No orders were received to retire, whether through oversight or design is not clear. As the afternoon wore on losses mounted. Among the wounded was Corporal James Gooding of the color guard. When darkness came, the Fifty-* *fourth was finally sent to the rear and the remnants of the regiment retreated in orderly fashion.*

Altogether the casualties from this battle were greater than those at Fort Wagner. A total of fifty-five officers and 1,806 men were killed, wounded, or missing. The Fifty-fourth recorded 86 casualties.[2]

[*Mercury*, February 15, 1864]

Hilton Head, Feb. 2, 1864

Messrs. Editors:—The heading of this letter is a sufficient intimation of our location. I should have written so as to catch the Atlantic, but the unavoidable confusion always attendant upon moving prevented my doing so. We have not been here long enough to know much about the place, and more than that, discipline is maintained so strictly that Uncle Sam's heroes are not permitted to run so loosely as they have been in the habit of doing. It seems as though we are just beginning to know how to play soldier. Being on Morris Island, working in the trenches and on the fortifications, where it would seem cruel to enforce the nicer points of order and military decorum, has made a wonderful change in the 54th, compared with regiments held under strict military surveillance. The boys don't like to see another regiment pluck the laurels off their brows, so they console themselves with the remark that "these 'ere fellers, with their bands and fine feathers, ain't been to Wagner yet." Some may say that the 54th has a rival; the 8th U.S. regiment is indeed a splendid organization, and I may add that no regiment in the

2. Ibid., 220. Emilio gives a total figure of 1,828, and for the 54th, three officers wounded, thirteen enlisted men killed, sixty-three wounded, and eight missing (*History of the Fifty-fourth*, 172–73). He calls it the bloodiest battle in which the Department of the South was engaged, saying that Seymour's tactics repeated his errors at Fort Wagner.

department can boast of a more healthy-looking, martial-bearing body of men; although in the manual of arms the old 54th can't be beat.[3]

Mutiny

There was quite a rumpus in the camp of the Independent Battalion, N.Y. Zouaves, on Saturday, caused by their refusal to be transferred to other regiments, their regiment being so depleted as to make such a course advisable. The difficulty was so great that it was necessary to plant two field pieces before them to bring them to reason. I believe the affair is satisfactorily cleared up, and the ringleaders are to be punished.

Bombardment

Our last recollections of Morris Island were vivified by a vigorous bombardment of something; for the big guns were blazing away in fine style as we lay in the inlet, on board the transports. Report says it was another pounding on Sumter, as the rebels had succeeded in mounting three guns there.

Snakes in Winter

Snakes are as abundant here now in February as they are North in July. We have killed no less than six since encamping here. The lizards are as plentiful as mosquitoes are in Jersey.

The Freedmen, Etc.

We have visits daily from the native population, who bring all sorts of little delicacies to sell, such as cakes, poultry, eggs, fruit and so

3. The 8th U.S. Colored Regiment was recently organized and newly arrived from the North (Emilio, *History of the Fifty-fourth*, 149).

on; but as the 54th is minus the circulating medium, they won't be enriched a great deal trading with us. Among the number are a great many women, who come merely to see and be seen; differing none in that respect from their sex in higher latitudes. Some of them too are good looking; and they know it too, for the dry goods dealers find out that these Southern ladies are very good customers. Another point is settled; the colored people down here seem to take as good care of themselves now as they did when they had "Massa" to look out for them, and it will be as natural as light follows darkness, that they will be no hindrance to labor in the North, so long as their wants are augmented by a state of freedom. The looms of New England will have employment weaving for these people, for their money will be as good to the manufacturers as that paid by others; and instead of emancipation being a losing operation, it will prove as it already begins to do, a commercial success. These people, who a year or so ago were slaves, are now the purchasers of such goods and clothes as their former masters and mistresses would be glad to see now; and it is a sure indication that if they have pride, or vanity if you will, to dress well, they will be equally industrious and frugal to secure the wherewith to purchase.

Aristocratic Peculiarities

Among the flocks of feminines, there came a young "she regiment" from Beaufort to see their long absent Pompeys, Abe Linkuns, Joe Unions, Fridays, Mondays, Washingtons, belonging to the 2d South Carolina volunteers, who have just arrived from the scene of active operations. There were all sorts of greetings, which were a little on the principle of New Zealand etiquette. Some of the pretty quondam waiting-maids had a holy horror of recognizing any one below the rank of a Sergeant, on the same principle perhaps, that the more favored ones of their sex go in for Brigadiers. One of these fine waiting-maid ladies, seeing a rather uncouth looking female salute her "Jake" with a friendly kiss, reproached Jake in this wise—"you Jake! you wipe you mouf off, you spose I kiss you gin, after Combee (Combahee) woman!"

Monitor

[*Mercury*, February 22, 1864]

Jacksonville, Fla., Feb. 8, 1864

Messrs. Editors:—I intimated in my hasty note of the 5th that we were off on another tramp, but with no knowledge of our destination. Yesterday afternoon the "Lincoln Gunboats" brought up before Jacksonville, so as to feel the way, before transports ventured up. At last the gunboats signalized that the way was clear, and the imposing fleet of steamers and vessels of all classes and sizes moved majestically up the St. John's river.[4] As we neared the town, say within three or four miles, the people along either bank of the river saluted the fleet by the waving of hats and handkerchiefs and other demonstrations of evident satisfaction. But as the long file of steamers swept by the town, preparing to near the docks, the women and children flocked to the wharves, or looked out of the windows, with a seemingly sullen silence—no waving of handkerchiefs greeted the old flag as it proudly floated from the peak of each vessel. It may be fairly presumed that the people of Jacksonville remember the heartless burning of their homes on a previous occupation by the Union forces. But Gen. Seymour is not the commander to tolerate the repetition of any such savagery.[5]

To resume; the flag steamer Mapleleaf had touched the dock, and some of the crew landed to make her fast, while the steamer "Gen. Hunter" about the same time touched another dock, when a volley of musketry was poured into the latter, wounding one of her mates, and one soldier, a member of the 54th Massachusetts regiment. The excitement on board the Hunter was at once intense—every man began to load without orders and rushed for the gangways to get on shore—and almost before those in command could give the necessary orders, the men were rushing pell-mell up through the streets, to catch, if possible, the cowardly crew who had fired on an unarmed transport. Major Appleton soon got off, with two companies, A and D, Capt. Grace in

4. Admiral Dahlgren had despatched the gunboats *Ottawa* and *Norwich* to escort the Union troops to Jacksonville (Emilio, *History of the Fifty-fourth*, 151).
5. Jacksonville was a key point in eastern Florida and had been occupied three times previously by Union troops (ibid., 153).

command of A, and Lieut. Durand, of D,[6] who moved at double-quick through the town till they came to the woods, when they deployed as skirmishers. The rebels retreated however, faster than our men could pursue, as the roads were obstructed by felled trees making a successful pursuit impossible. The detachment from the 54th captured 13 prisoners, and those from the 1st Mass. cavalry 5, with a horse, cart and a little booty, about three miles from the town. Seven companies of the former regiment were posted as advanced pickets, supported by a detachment of mounted rifles from the 40th Mass.

We are now encamped half a mile from the town, with the 47th and 48th New York, and the 8th U.S., waiting for the artillery to debark before proceeding on the march into the interior.

The faces of the ladies in Jacksonville indicated a sort of Parisian disgust as the well-appointed Union army, composed in part of Lincoln's "niggers," filed through the streets. I am happy to say, that the 54th behaved in the most exemplary manner—not a low jest was indulged as they passed through the streets, in most cases lined with women. A respectful silence was maintained by the men, some of whom have experienced the misfortune of being black by the treatment they have received from those now in rebellion. To-day those, who at first greeted us with frowns, are treating us with respect and courtesy; in fact more than we should expect to receive in some parts of the free North. And that respect is not due to the presence of an overwhelming army—lasting only so long as cannon are ranged on their homes—but respect paid to men who by their deportment show that they are christianized, if not very refined.

10th—Our forces were in motion at 12 M., of the 8th, following the railway, and at 7 P.M., captured a rebel battery of five pieces, the rebels skedaddling, and the 4[0]th Mass. in hot pursuit. The vanguard rushed into a rebel camp last night and captured a whole company under

6. This was Charles Maltby Duren of Cambridge, Mass., whose letters describing the Florida campaign were published as "The Occupation of Jacksonville, February 1864, and the Battle of Olustee," *Florida Historical Quarterly* 32 (1953–54): 262–87. In one letter Duren writes, "If you can get a 'New Bedford Mercury' Feb. 26—you will find an article in relation to this expedition to Florida speaks of Lieut. Durand with his Co. landing first etc.—One of the officers saw the paper—I knew nothing of it—" (278).

command of a lieutenant. The prisoners were brought down to Jacksonville this afternoon in two cars drawn by mules, as the engines on the road have been purposely damaged to prevent our using them. At last accounts, the right of our column was beyond Pilatka, having met with no strenuous opposition as yet.

Monitor

[*Mercury*, March 9, 1864]

Jacksonville, Fla., Feb. 25, 1864

Messrs. Editors:—I am pained to inform you that Corporal James H. Gooding was killed in battle on the 20th inst. at Olustee Station. He was one of the Color Corporals and was with the colors at the time. So great was the rout of our troops that we left nearly all our dead and wounded on the field. The fight lasted four hours. We were badly beaten that night, and the next day we kept falling back, until we reached Jacksonville. The fifty-fourth did honor to themselves and our city. All concede that no regiment fought like it.

James H. Buchanan, of New Bedford, was killed; and Sergeant Wharton A. William, also of our city, was wounded in the hand. Many others of Co. C were wounded; but none of them from our city.

The regiment is pleased to learn that the bill to pay them $13 per month passed.

The total loss of the regiment, I am unable to give you at this time. All we want now is more troops; with them we would go forward again and drive the rebels from the State.

Your friend/James W. Grace/Captain Fifty-Fourth Regiment

Epilogue

A word about the terrible defeat in Florida. . . . The rebels allowed us to penetrate, and then, with ten to our one, cut us off, meaning to 'bag' us. And had it not been for the glorious Fifty-fourth Massachusetts, the whole brigade would have been captured or annihilated. This was the only regiment that rallied, broke the rebel ranks, and saved us. The 8th United States Colored lost their flag twice, and the Fifty-fourth recaptured it each time. They have lost in killed and missing about 350. They would not retreat when ordered, but charged on them with the most fearful desperation. . . . If this regiment has not won glory enough to have shoulder straps, where is there one that ever did.[7]

7. This epilogue is an extract from a letter from Beaufort, dated Feb. 26, from "a gentleman who accompanied General Seymour" (*The Liberator*, March 18, 1864, 47).

Appendix A

Correspondence on the Issue of Equal Pay

There was nothing that more clearly reflected the prejudices of society at large or the ambivalence of the United States government toward its black troops than the matter of pay. When the War Department authorized the recruitment of southern blacks for military duty in August 1862, they were "to be entitled to, and receive, the same pay and rations as are allowed, by law, to volunteers in the service."[1] Later Governor Andrew received a similar promise for any regiments raised in Massachusetts.[2]

Yet the Militia Act, passed on July 17, 1862, specified that blacks were to be paid $10.00 per month minus $3.00 deducted for clothing. White soldiers, on the other hand, received $10.00 per month plus a clothing allowance. The law reflected the government's initial plan to recruit among the newly freed slaves or "contrabands" and to use them in noncombat roles as laborers, kitchen personnel, and camp guards.

When the United States Bureau of Colored Troops was organized in May 1863, Secretary of War Stanton asked his legal adviser for a ruling on the pay of colored soldiers and was told that by law their pay would have to be the lesser amount.[3]

At St. Helena Island, the Fifty-fourth Regiment was mustered for pay on June 30 and first heard about the ruling. Colonel Shaw wrote in protest to Governor Andrew on July 2 saying, "In my opinion they should be mustered out of the service or receive the full pay which was promised them. The paymaster here is inclined to class us with the contraband regiments, and pay the men only $10. If he does not change his mind, I shall refuse to have the regiment paid until I hear from you on the subject."[4]

After the battle of Fort Wagner,

1. Quoted in Wilson, *Black Phalanx*, 133.
2. Fox, *Record of . . . Fifty-Fifth Mass. Infantry*, 86.
3. McPherson, *Negro's Civil War*, 196–97.
4. Quoted in Emilio, *History of the Fifty-fourth*, 48.

when Shaw's regiment had shown its mettle under fire for the second time, the men refused the United States paymaster's offer of the lesser sum. By this time the regiment had been without pay for several months and their families at home were suffering. Nevertheless the men also turned down Massachusetts' offer to make up the difference. Their self-respect demanded equal treatment from the government which had promised it to them.

Early the next year, Senator Henry Wilson of Massachusetts introduced legislation for the retroactive equalization of pay, but it was not until mid-June 1864 that the law, heavily compromised, was finally passed. Three months later, on September 28 and 29, the

United States paymaster distributed $170,000 in back pay to the men of the Fifty-fourth Regiment.[5] It had come too late for Henry Gooding.

The first letter below was written by Gooding to President Lincoln in the fall of 1863 and sent by way of the Harper Brothers office in New York City. There is no evidence in the Lincoln Papers or in the National Archives, where Gooding's letter is kept, to indicate that the president ever saw it. The letters that follow are exchanges between James B. Congdon of New Bedford and Governor Andrew in which Congdon forwards the communications he has received from Gooding on the pay question.

Camp of the 54th Mass. Colored Regt. Morris Island.

Dept of the South. Sept. 28th, 1863.

Your Excellency, Abraham Lincoln:

Your Excellency will pardon the presumption of an humble individual like myself, in addressing you, but the earnest Solicitation of my Comrades in Arms beside the genuine interest felt by myself in the matter is my excuse, for placing before the Executive head of the Nation our Common Grievance.

On the 6th of the last Month, the Paymaster of the department

5. Ibid., 227–28.

informed us, that if we would decide to receive the sum of $10 (ten dollars) per month, he would come and pay us that sum, but that, on the sitting of Congress, the Regt. would, in his opinion, be allowed the other 3 (three). He did not give us any guarantee that this would be, as he hoped; certainly he had no authority for making any such guarantee, and we cannot suppose him acting in any way interested.

Now the main question is, Are we Soldiers, or are we Labourers? We are fully armed, and equipped, have done all the various Duties pertaining to a Soldier's life, have conducted ourselves to the complete satisfaction of General Officers, who were, if any[thing], prejudiced against us, but who now accord us all the encouragement and honour due us; have shared the perils and Labour of Reducing the first stronghold that flaunted a Traitor Flag; and more, Mr. President. Today the Anglo-Saxon Mother, Wife, or Sister are not alone in tears for departed Sons, Husbands and Brothers. The patient, trusting Descendants of Afric's Clime have dyed the ground with blood, in defense of the Union, and Democracy. Men, too, your Excellency, who know in a measure the cruelties of the Iron heel of oppression, which in years gone by, the very Power their blood is now being spilled to maintain, ever ground them to the dust.

But When the war trumpet sounded o'er the land, when men knew not the Friend from the Traitor, the Black man laid his life at the Altar of the Nation,—and he was refused. When the arms of the Union were beaten, in the first year of the War, and the Executive called [for] more food for its ravaging [ravenous?] maw, again the black man begged the privilege of aiding his Country in her need, to be again refused.

And now he is in the War, and how has he conducted himself? Let their dusky forms rise up, out [of] the mires of James Island, and give the answer. Let the rich mould around Wagner's parapets be upturned, and there will be found an Eloquent answer. Obedient and patient and Solid as a wall are they. All we lack is a paler hue and a better acquaintance with the Alphabet.

Now your Excellency, we have done a Soldier's Duty. Why Can't we have a Soldier's pay? You caution the Rebel Chieftain, that the United States knows no distinction in her Soldiers. She insists on having all her Soldiers of whatever creed or Color, to be treated according to the usages of War. Now if the United States exacts uniformity of treatment of her Soldiers from the Insurgents, would it not be well and consistent to set the example herself by paying all her Soldiers alike?

We of this Regt. were not enlisted under any "contraband" act. But we do not wish to be understood as rating our Service of more Value to the Government than the service of the ex-slave. Their Service is undoubtedly worth much to the Nation, but Congress made express provision touching their case, as slaves freed by military necessity, and assuming the Government to be their temporary Guardian. Not so with us. Freemen by birth and consequently having the advantage of thinking and acting for ourselves so far as the Laws would allow us, we do not consider ourselves fit subject for the Contraband act.

We appeal to you, Sir, as the Executive of the Nation, to have us justly Dealt with. The Regt. do pray that they be assured their service will be fairly appreciated by paying them as American Soldiers, not as menial hirelings. Black men, you may well know, are poor; three dollars per month for a year will supply their needy Wives and little ones with fuel. If you, as Chief Magistrate of the Nation, will assure us of our whole pay, we are content. Our Patriotism, our enthusiasm will have a new impetus, to exert our energy more and more to aid our Country. Not that our hearts ever flagged in Devotion, spite the evident apathy displayed in our behalf, but We feel as though our Country spurned us, now that we are sworn to serve her. Please give this a moment's attention. [signed] James Henry Gooding.[6]

On August 20, 1863, James B. Congdon wrote to Governor Andrew as follows:

Dear Sir,

I have sent you an extract from a letter I have just received from a member of Co. C 54th. I have only to say that I know the writer well. He belongs in this city, and many of his letters from the camp and the army have been published in the N. B. Mercury. He is intelligent, honest, patriotic.

Ever and most Truly yours,
James B. Congdon

6. National Archives, Record Group No. 94, Colored Troops Division, Letters Received, H133, CT 1863.

[*The extract*]

Extract from a letter from James Henry Gooding, a non-commissioned officer of Company C 54th Regt. dated August 13th, 1863.

After speaking of the murders by the mob in New York while the race to which the victims belonged were fighting and bleeding on Morris Island, he says, "another point to which I would call your attention is the effort to put the regiment off with ten dollars a month. Comment is unnecessary by me. Suffice it to say, the regiment in a body refused to take it. As it was an act of option with us to take it or wait till the government took some further action in the matter, we chose to wait. As our State made no distinction in raising the 54th and paying the aid appropriated we expect the General Government to treat us at least justly. If we are wrong in not accepting it, it is not because we are prone to do wrong for wrong's sake, but because we were doing the best for our own protection against fraud."[7]

At the beginning of December 1863, the following letters were exchanged.

To His Excellency John A. Andrew, Governor.

Dear Sir,

I enclose a copy of a letter I have this day received from James H. Gooding, a non-commissioned officer of company C. 54th regiment. I believe I have once before sent you a portion of his correspondence. Mr. Gooding is shrewd and intelligent.

I am not aware that any importance is to be attached to this communication, but I have thought it well to place it in your hands.

With high Regards
James B. Congdon

New Bedford Dec. 14, 1863

Copy   Morris Island, Nov. 29, 1863

James B. Congdon Esq.

Dear Sir,

I beg to acknowledge the receipt of your favors of the 16th and 18th instants, respectively.

---

7. Massachusetts Archives at Columbia Point, Executive Department Letters, 1862–1864, vol. 59, no. 17.

I hope you will pardon my brevity, but I must plead want of time as my excuse.

My dear Sir, you have made too much of my poor sentiments as set forth in my letter to yourself on the 9th instant. I never dreamed that there was anything striking in a man's expression of loyalty in a crisis like this, and yours and the Hon. A. H. Bullock's seeming commendation of my loyalty is truly flattering. But enough of that.

I see a little speck in the horizon: if I can through some sound and influential friends of the cause avert it before it assumes a larger shape I would. The men of the regiment do not understand the terms of the Governor's message in regard to the payment of this and the 55th regiments.

I fear that this sense of dignity, exhibited by the regiment in refusing ten dollars from the Government, is being carried too far. They claim, that the State, in paying the deficiency refused by the General Government, is virtually upholding the Government in its injustice. To my mind this is not the fact. So long as they have shewn that they know the difference between fair play and foul, surely their dignity is safe enough, even by accepting the ten dollars from the Government under protest.

Now, I advise that the message of the Governor be sent to the men, say a thousand copies, with an exposition of the plainest possible language, that they may know that the State means to do justly, not act to please their vanity or dignity.

The African race are naturally suspicious, arising from ignorance, they are to be dealt with cautiously. You will readily appreciate my motives.

Signed   James Henry Gooding[8]

Commonwealth of Massachusetts/Executive Department
Boston. Decr. 20th, 1863.
James B. Congdon, Esqr./New Bedford. Mass.
My dear Sir:

I thank you for your letter and the copy of Sergt. Gooding's. While I fully appreciate his intelligence and good will, I can only say that I

8. Ibid., no. 92.

have no time for the effort to explain to those who do not understand what is so clear. Those two regiments had, and have, to my mind, the clear right to be treated, in all respects, both by national and State governments as soldiers of the Union, nothing less, nor more. The U.S. treated them, in respect to their pay as something less, an act, (as I think I shewed in my recent address to the Legislature) not warranted by the law of the U.S. itself. I regard this act of the U.S. authorities as a mistake in law, as well as in justice and policy. Massachusetts could not compel the United States government to adopt our opinions. We could only use our influence. I did this by talking with the President, the Judge Advocate Genl. of the Army—(Judge Holt), and with the Secretary at War, the Secretary of State and the Secretary of the Treasury,—as fully and clearly as I could, explaining and urging my views, and besides that filing a written argument on the subject.

My address to the Legislature contains an argument to shew that by the law of the U.S. the government has no right to discriminate between soldiers of the same rank; that neither birth nor color create grounds of distinction.

If the U.S. Government would not yield to our view, or delayed to do so, there were two things still remaining, besides endeavoring to get Congress to correct the error; viz—

1st   To emphasise, in the strongest way our expression of the self of injustice created in our minds by this discrimination made against the colored men.

2nd   To do all we could to render that discrimination less burdensome, by sharing the burden of it ourselves with the colored soldiers whom we had raised. How could even the ingenuity of suspicion torture into the most latent [blatant?] toleration of the distinction made against colored men, an act of our State government by which the pay of our soldiers was assumed and offered by the Commonwealth, on the very ground and for the very reason that its refusal by the U.S. was wrong. We said: The U.S. is wrong; and while they delay to right, we, for the sake of justice and our own honor, will volunteer to do the right instead. Can anything be more clear? I respect the manly feeling which suggested to these soldiers the refusal of the money from us; if they felt it tended to strengthen the cause of their race before Congress. But, it is plain that, there would have been no want of dignity in their accepting it as an advance made by Mass., which it was, in the faith that the law of the U.S. would be so amended by Congress as to put their case beyond doubt or cavil.—I am yours truly & respectfully—

John A. Andrew[9]

9. Andrew, Letters Sent, 1861–1865, 18: 392–95.

Appendix B

Six Poems Composed at Sea by Henry Gooding

The following six poems by Henry Gooding may all have been written on Gooding's first voyage in the bark *Sunbeam*, 1856–1859. The deep feelings generated by a long separation from family and familiar surroundings, the loneliness, the recognition of ever present danger and the possibility of death would have been experienced most keenly by a green hand at sea for the first time. On board a whaleship there were long periods of relative inactivity and a sensitive youth with literary interests would have time for writing poetry.

Approaching the poems with this in mind, one can almost see the order in which they might have been written. "The Sailor Boy's Song" would come first, with its exuberance and offhand references to danger and death "'neath the dark blue sea." In "The Sailor's Thoughts of Home" the poet begins to feel loneliness and a certain regret at having left home, realizing that "three long years must pass, / E'er I shall see them more."

Next might come the poem "In Memory of Eli Dodge" in which Gooding's earlier feelings on the loss of his shipmate are heightened by the tragedy of Dodge's death. No longer can the poet sentimentalize death at sea. In "The Sailor's Regret" he writes, "Oh bury me not 'neath the wide rolling billow, / Where the wild sea bird will cry over me / But let me lay 'neath the old weeping willow, / Far, far away from the tempestuous sea."

"Reply to a Friend's Counsels" seems to have been written as the voyage ended. There is the hint that Gooding's relations with his family, particularly his father, were strained, but that Gooding had hoped, in vain, to hear from them during the voyage. In the last verse, the poet acknowledges that despite his estrangement from his family, their prayers and good wishes have brought him home safely. The "friend" of the title may be his mother, whose counsels are mentioned, or perhaps a shipmate who has advised Gooding to attempt reconciliation.

The poem that is difficult to fit into this pattern is "'Twas Not My Own Native Land." This poem, if autobiographical, recounts a period in Gooding's life for which there is no other documentation. Not one of Gooding's three voyages between 1856 and 1862 could have taken him to the Near East, Italy, Greece, Germany, Spain, France, and/or England. It is possible, but I think it unlikely, that these wanderings occurred before Gooding arrived in New Bedford at the age of nineteen. What seems most possible is that the poem is a work of pure imagination by someone who had read widely about the travel of others.

Like other whalemen who wrote poetry, Gooding was influenced by the literary trends of his day. This was a period when the popular press was rapidly developing. Amateurs in all genres were filling newspapers and magazines with their prose and poetry, much of it pompous, sentimental, and less than second-rate. Among whalemen, favorite themes were home, love, loneliness, and death, and, according to one writer, their efforts "can scarcely be separated from that which was being written on shore."[1]

Gooding's poems, printed in broadside format on thin paper, were given to the Old Dartmouth Historical Society in 1916 by Frank E. Brown, a New Bedford manufacturer of whaling gear in the final years of the industry. They are previously unrecorded and possibly unique; they do not appear in the *National Union Catalog*, the comprehensive Harris Collection of American poetry at Brown University, or in the broadside collection of the American Antiquarian Society.

The circumstances under which the poems may have been printed is not known. Their typography is similar to work done at the Mercury Job Printing Office in New Bedford. Perhaps Gooding had a few copies printed for distribution among family and friends upon his return. Perhaps after Gooding's death someone arranged for the poems to be printed and sold for the benefit of his widow. So far the facts of the case have eluded discovery.[2]

---

1. Pamela Miller, *And the Whale Is Ours: Creative Writing of American Whalemen* (Boston, 1979), 16, 175. Miller's survey did not identify any African-American writers (3).

2. If Gooding was briefly employed at the *Mercury* before enlisting, he may have printed the poems himself. Their typography suggests inexperience.

The Sailor Boy's Song
Composed at Sea

Youth.
Oh the land is a dull place now to me,
I long to roam o'er the dark blue sea,
Where the winds do blow and the seas roll high,
Oh, there is the home of a Sailor Boy.

Maid.
Risk not thy life upon the sea,
But stay, love, at home; Oh! do for me,—
And drink of bliss without aloy,
For hard is the life of a Sailor Boy.

Youth.
The land looks bright but I cannot stay,
See, my barque awaits to bear me away,
I'll leave my home and every joy,
To lead the gay life of a Sailor Boy.

'Twill be my pride when on the sea,
To add my mite to the sailor's glee,
To share each danger or mount on high,
When duty calls on the Sailor Boy.

Then if grim death should call for me,
My grave should be 'neath the dark blue sea,
Where winds with the waves sport like a toy,
Oh that's the last wish of a Sailor Boy.

The Sailor's Thoughts of Home
Composed at Sea

How long and sad, the time does seem,
As lone the deck I pace,
And think of some sweet childhood's dream,
Which time can ne'er efface.

To think of the dear loved, as
I roam from shore to shore;
And think that three long years must pass,
E'er I shall see them more.

And think how often I have play'd
Beneath the old oak tree;
And think if home I would have stay'd
How happy I should be.

And think how often I have roam'd
All through the grassy mead,
Near my dear, sweet native home,
The time seems long indeed.

If unto them the time does seem
As long as 'tis to me,
They then must think of me in dreams,
While I am on the sea.

Must count the weary hours, as they
Do think of me by night,
And watch with rapture for the day
That I shall greet their sight.

In Memory of Eli Dodge, Who Was Killed by a Whale

Sept. 4, 1858, off the Coast of New Holland
Composed at Sea

He has gone from our gaze, he'll never more return
A shipmate we all did revere,
We no more of him, our duty will learn,
No more with us, will he make cheer.

He had perhaps a dear cottage home,
Or maybe a sister or a brother,
Who knows but a wife,
The joy of his life,
A child, or a fond loving mother.

He was brave in the storm,
He was kind in the calm,
His duty he done like a man,
But now he is free from this world's alarms,
And safe moor'd in the Spirit land.

He ofttimes with us did the monster pursue,
The huge monster king of the deep,
But now he is gone, and his journey is through,
Where loud billows roll he does sleep.

How little we thought, but a moment before,
When near us he bravely did contend,
With the huge monster then weltering in its gore,
That he would to hades Eli send.

But he's gone from our gaze, his long race is run,
In death's cold embrace he does lie,
Yet Father of Mercies Thy will be done,
And take his soul to Thee on High.

The Sailor's Regret
Composed at Sea

Oh, bury me not 'neath the wide rolling billow,
Where the wild seabird will cry over me,
But let me lay 'neath the old weeping willow,
Far, far away from the tempestuous sea.

Oh, let me lay near my departed sires,
In the old churchyard, where wild flowers grow,
So that at eve, when the sun it retires,
Friends, they may gaze where I am laid so low.

Oh, bury me not where the wild ocean's foaming,
Where hollow winds unceasing do roar;
But take, Oh, take me when I am done roaming,
And lay me down on my own native shore.

For there dwells my loved one, Oh! there dwells my mother,
There dwells all on earth that to me is dear;
There is my father, my sister and brother,
Within their dear gaze Oh, do lay me near.

Well do I know that many a wild rover,
Has craved a grave 'neath the wide rolling deep,
But as for me, when this weary life is over,
In my own native land I want to sleep.

Reply to a Friend's Counsels
Composed at Sea

'Tis true, I have been o'er the wide rolling billow,
And thought the long night, as I've watched for the morn,
I've longed to lay down on that long cherished pillow,
Where safe I would be from the rain and the storm.

And when far away, I remember that Mother,
Who, well do I know, was then weeping for me,
Who tried, but in vain, her forebodings to smother,
That danger was near her dear boy on the sea.

Her counsels, Oh, think you I e'er could forget them?
When stamped they were deeply imbuded in my breast,
When on her bent knees, she was imploring Heaven,
To shield me, and guide, to a haven of rest.

My author of being, forgot him, Oh! never,
For fear his grey hairs would be brought low by shame,
Of a son void of gratitude, who would thus sever
The link of affection, God's own holy chain.

My own native home, of thee I've often thought,
And brothers, and sisters, that to me are dear,
I've wished, but in vain, and time never brought,
A moment of comfort, or one word of cheer.

Your wishes and prayers have proved wherever dwelling,
On land or on oceans propitious to me,
And prospering breezes the white canvass swelling,
Has brought me in safety from over the sea.

'Twas Not My Own Native Land
Composed at Sea

I have wandered afar in bright eastern climes,
I have listened with pleasure to sweet vesper chimes;
But soft as clime, as bright were the sands,
I felt that it was not my own native land.
Oh no, 'twas not my own native land.

When I gazed with mute wonder on proud Minarets,
Or sat in the noontide near bright sparkling jets,
And saw the meek Pilgrims assembling in bands,
I felt that it was not my own native land.

I've trod where Vesuvius threw her volumes of fire,
And gazed where proud Pompeii once reared her tall spires,
I've strolled through learned Athens, through chivalrous Rome,
But I felt not as if in my own native home.

I've journeyed delighted on the romantic Rhine,
And gazed on proud castles laid low by old Time,
Saw fair blue-eyed maidens with smiles sweet and bland,
But they seemed not so fair as the maids of my land.

I've travelled through bright Andalusia's famed land,
The land famed in story for bold pirate bands,
I've seen the escurial with gold crested dome,
But it lured me not from my own native home.

I've drank deep of pleasure in gay sunny France,
And joined with brave gallants and maids in the dance,
And proud stately ladies with soft jewelled hands,
But I felt not as if in my own native land.

I've wandered through Merry Old England's proud halls,
Where green ivy's creeping all o'er their great walls,
But I longed for my home beyond her white strand,
I longed for my home in my own native land.

Index

Stephens, Alexander H., 49
Stevenson, Gen. Thomas G., 36–37,
  56
Stone, Lincoln R., 12
Stone Fleet, 61
Stono River, 36 n
Strong, Brig. Gen. George C., 38,
  77 n
Strong, Fort. *See* Wagner, Fort
Substitutes, 86
Sullivan's Island, 34, 60, 67, 68, 71,
  75, 81, 89
Sumter, Fort, xviii, 34, 71, 81–82,
  90 n; attack on, 59, 77; bombard-
  ment of, 44, 52, 56, 59, 65, 73–75,
  76–77, 78, 80, 83, 89–90, 110
Sunbeam (whaling bark), xxiii–xxv,
  125
Swails, Sgt. Stephen A., xxviii n,
  xxxii
"Swamp Angel" (gun), 60

Telegraph, 81
Terry, Brig. Gen. Alfred H., 37, 56
Thanksgiving Day, 85–86
Thompson, Captain, 28
Toombs, Robert, 60
Torrance, Abram P., 42, 46
Toussaint Guards, xxx
Troy, N.Y., xxii, xxxii–xxxiii

Uniforms, 5
United States Army regiments, 55 n,
  79, 95, 97, 109, 110 n, 113, 115
United States Bureau of Colored
  Troops, 117
United States Navy, xxvii

Vallandigham, Clement L., 64
Van Allen, Charles, 58
Vanderpoel, Alexander, 55

Vattel, Emerich de, 63
Virginia, C.S.S. See *Merrimack*
Visitors to camp, 11, 15, 16–17, 20,
  21, 24, 110–11
Vogelsgang, Peter, xxviii n

Wagner (Strong), Fort, xi, xii, xiii,
  35, 60, 65, 66, 72, 73, 74, 77, 82,
  84, 89, 90, 95, 99; first assault on,
  35–36; second assault on, 38–40;
  occupied, 45, 56–57; siege of, 45–
  47, 51–56
Wampanoags, xix
Wardrobe, Colonel, 30
Warren, Joseph, 98
Wars of earlier centuries, 101
Washington, Charles, 107
Weapons, 16, 57, 60, 65, 68, 82
Weather, 10, 33, 55, 61, 90, 106
Webster, Thomas, 104 n
Weehawken (U.S. monitor), 33 n, 87–
  88, 91
Welch, Sgt. Frank M., xxviii n, 100
Welles, Gideon, 94
West Indians, xx, xxi
*Whalemen's Shipping List and Mer-
  chants Transcript*, xxvi
Whaling and blacks, xix–xxi
Whitworth guns, 45
William and Mary, king and queen of
  England, 101
Williams, Sgt. Wharton A., 20, 114
Wilson, Pvt. George, xxxii
Wilson, Henry, 118
Wilson, Pvt. Joseph T., 107
Wilson, Sgt. Joseph D., 37
Wood, Fernando, 31
Wyley, James, 30

Yankee character, 66, 70
Young, Pvt. Nathan L., 46